MY DAUGHTERS ARE TRYING TO KILL ME... BUT I LOVE THEM ANYWAY

Stories From A Father of Autistic Daughters

BARNABY DICKENSON

My Daughters Are Trying To Kill Me... But I Love Them Anyway

ISBN 9798488606852

First Published 2021

Copyright © Barnaby Dickenson 2021

The moral right of the author has been asserted

Instagram: barnabyauthor
Twitter: @BarnabyAuthor
Email: barnjarn@me.com

Cover Design: Oliver Bennet - More Visual Ltd

Cover Photos: Jade Langton Evans

For Karen

'If I know what love is, it is because of you.'

CHAPTERS

As a huge music lover, I gave every chapter and blog post a song title. I chose titles that, for me, summed up the feeling of the chapter or post. Some of my favourite singers and songs are represented, but inclusion of a song title should not always be taken as an endorsement of its musical merits. Libby does love 'Escape (The Pina Colada Song)' as it's in Shrek, but I'm not a huge fan of Deacon Blue ('Chocolate Girl').

HOW TO READ THIS BOOK

If you've picked up this book and are hoping for a forensic and academic analysis of autism, then put the book down now and walk away; this is not the book for you. If, however, you would like to read stories that are both hysterically funny and, at times, heartbreakingly sad, about two wonderful autistic girls and their rather exhausted parents, then stay.

I have no formal qualifications that would make me a suitable person to write an analytical book about autism, but then, this isn't primarily a book on that subject. It's a book about Robyn and Liberty; our beautiful, clever, funny and, at times, utterly exasperating daughters, who also happen to be autistic. So, let me say this once in the hope that it will suffice:

I am *not* an expert in autism; I *am* an expert on my daughters.

This is very much a book written by a layman in the area of autism, though I have over 20 years of fieldwork experience through caring for our autistic children, so I'm not exactly a novice in this area, either. It's certainly true that many people know more about autism than me, but no one knows my daughters as well as I do, other than my wife, Karen, who I respect as the ultimate authority on all things Robyn and Liberty.

Now, 'How To Read This Book'; I do have some guidance in order for you to follow the narrative. The beginnings of this book go back to January 2011 when, as a vague New Year's resolution, I decided to write a blog about my daughters and, over the course of the year, I wrote about 25 posts. By the end of the year I felt I had told the stories I wanted to tell, and that was that. People I knew would bring the blog up in conversation from time to time and they would always ask two questions:

1. Are you going to write any more?
2. Are you going to turn it into a book?

For a long time, the answers were 'no' and 'no'. Then, earlier this year, I decided to say 'yes' and 'yes'. I had the idea of publishing the blogs, and then adding to the original posts with updates and lots of newer stories about our girls from the last 10 years. The book is not written chronologically; instead, the chapters are loosely themed on subjects such as communication, dangerous behaviour, and food. Basically:

When you see a block of writing in italics, it will be a blog post from 2011.

Everything not in italics was written in 2021.

Just one acknowledgement before I let you get on with reading our stories. When I wrote the blog posts back in 2011, I wrote about the girls, of course, but I also make fairly frequent references to our eldest child, George, who is not autistic. In the last year or two, George has become G and identifies as non-binary. When the stories in this book took place, they were still George, and I was concerned that changing their identity in only some places might be confusing for some readers. G has very graciously allowed me to refer to them throughout the book as George, and I am grateful to them for their understanding. Love you, G.

THE MOMENT I KNEW

BLOG POST FROM FEBRUARY 6 2011 - NEW
BEGINNING (MAMBA SEYRA)

*A*ccepted wisdom among film critics is that Chris Nolan's comic book epic 'The Dark Knight' is a better film than the film that preceded it, 'Batman Begins'. The reason they give for this, amongst others, is that it's generally accepted that 'origin stories' aren't very interesting. Apparently, the audience doesn't want to see the back story of why mild-mannered Bruce Wayne becomes Batman; we just want to see Batman kicking some evil villain tail.

Respectfully, film critic guys, I disagree. I prefer Batman Begins to The Dark Knight (and so does Mark Kermode, so I'm not on my own). You see, I like a good origin story. I like to know how things came to be; I like to know why an ordinary billionaire decides he must become a borderline psycho, ass-kicking vigilante.

So, I'm thinking that maybe you'll agree with me enough for me to tell you our origin story. I'm hoping that you don't just want to read entertaining yarns about poo, although you'll get plenty of those, too. I also think, though, that this story may be too long for one bite-size blog. Let's call this Part One of the origin story. 'Robyn Begins', if you will.

Like many autistic kids I've read about, Robyn developed just fine for 18 months. Those who know her have fond memories of a beautiful little toddler who would say 'Mum', 'Dad' and 'Georgie' (her brother). My mum always talks about how she remembers, back in 1999, Robyn singing 'Once Upon A Dream' from Disney's Sleeping Beauty. I remember it, too. It's a memory that stings the back of my eyes whenever I recall it. I can still see her in my mind's eye, standing in front of the television at my mum's house, swaying from side to side as she sang along with perfect pitch and half formed words. She says nothing now. Nothing intelligible, at least.

Even when things started to get strange, she used to talk a little. When they were tiny, George and Robyn shared bunk beds in our two bedroom house. George would fall asleep but Robyn would lie awake, laughing. Not a small chuckle, but a giggle, like someone was tickling her. Then she would say in a singsong voice, 'Georgie, where are you? Yee-ha', and make a clicking sound. Karen and I would lie in bed listening to her and smiling at how odd our little girl was, but not worrying too much. After all, she seemed healthy and happy; what two year old isn't a little bit strange?

As time went on, there were more and more clues that things weren't right. The talking decreased, until all we got was the occasional 'bye-bye'; and the repetitive behaviour and insular play increased, until all she seemed to do was line toys up and take them down again. I remember exactly the first time that someone said the A-word to me in regards to Robyn. I was talking with someone at church, who was a nurse, and I was describing Robyn's behaviour. She looked at me and said, in a fairly off-hand way; 'Have you ever thought she might be autistic?'

It's easy to be wise after the event and pretend you knew something when you didn't. Well-meaning family and friends would tell us at the time that Robyn was fine, that she was just experiencing some developmental delay, that one day she would just start talking. And I didn't even know much about autism outside of 'Rainman'. But in the moment she said 'autistic', I knew. For me, it was just a matter of time before a diagnosis was given.

Robyn, aged 2. She was stunning, but that far away
look was a clue as to what was to come.

BLOG POST FROM MARCH 4 2011 - ESCAPE (THE PINA COLADA SONG)

As Dickens famously wrote in A Tale of Two Cities, it was the best of times; it was the worst of times. Except, in our case, the bit about it being the best of times is a complete lie. However, one of the worst nights of my life did end up having some positive aspects.

If I remember correctly, it was early in the year 2000. Robyn would have been about to turn two and George was nearly four. Karen had gone out for the evening and was over at a friend's house, leaving me at home with our two young children. I like to think that I'm a reasonably capable dad; not the sort of dad that his wife has to worry every time she leaves him with the kids in case there's a huge disaster. Except that this night was, by any reasonable measure of the word, pretty disastrous.

Early on in the evening I was working on the computer, which was in our bedroom, and Robyn was playing in her bedroom across the small landing. After a few minutes I went downstairs, leaving Robyn to play in her room. So I thought.

The irony of this situation is that I remember being a good dad that night. George and I sat together watching Crufts on television, laughing at the pampered pets doing those doggie assault courses. Then we played a Disney board game together and I let George win. In fact, I was enjoying being a good dad with George so much that I forgot that Robyn was playing upstairs on her own and I hadn't checked on her for half an hour. But I did remember eventually and went upstairs to make sure she was OK. She wasn't there.

We lived in a classic 'two up, two down' terraced house at the time – a grand total of six rooms. And I spent the next 45 minutes looking for Robyn in our house. 45 long minutes looking through six small rooms. It was that night that I learned the power of denial. I kept looking and looking because Robyn had to be there. She had to be there because the alternative was just too awful to contemplate.

After I had searched in every conceivable place half a dozen times, I had to face the truth. Robyn was missing and she'd been gone for well over an hour. While I had been in my room for a few minutes on the computer, she had left her room, gone straight down the stairs and straight out of the front door. I thought she was still there the whole time. I called Karen who then called the police. Robyn had been found wandering along the busy main road near our house. It was dark and cold and she wasn't properly dressed. Two boys had taken her to a house on the road and the woman who lived there called the police. Robyn seemed perfectly happy at this complete stranger's house, and when Karen and the police arrived to pick her up, she was sitting on the stairs enjoying a drink the lady had made for her.

Karen and the police arrived at our house and the police invited themselves in. Any parent can imagine how I felt. There was a vague sense of relief that she was safe, but a gut wrenching sickness in my stomach as I contemplated the possibilities of what could have happened. The police, with the brilliant people skills that they have been trained to use in such circumstances, thought that what the situation clearly called for was to give this distraught dad an almighty rollicking. 'She could be dead!' shouted the police officer. Really? Thanks for pointing that out because it actually hadn't crossed my mind...

Then, Social Services arrived. And this, believe it or not, is where the story becomes more positive. Unlike with the police, we were able to explain to the Social Services people how we had already been concerned about Robyn's behaviour, which was strange even for a two-year-old. They agreed that a child leaving home and wandering off to a stranger's house without showing the least sign of distress was unusual. Far from calling at our house to take our kids away from us, this was the beginning of getting the help and support that we needed to help us to cope with Robyn's (and later Liberty's) autism. Had Robyn not escaped that night we would have had more of a struggle to get the diagnosis; a situation that the parents of many autistic children experience. Social Services involvement at an early stage actually helped to speed up this process.

Eventually, sometime around midnight, Social Services left the house. I sat down next to Karen on the settee and cried like I hadn't cried since I was a little kid myself. Big, uncontrollable sobs.

I'd love to tell you that writing this post has been cathartic and rewarding but, truth be told, I feel waves of nausea as I remember the events of that night. I can vividly recall the feeling of sickening fear of not knowing where our child was, followed by the emotion of shame and embarrassment that Robyn had gone missing on my watch. I was a bad parent. I must be; the police had said so.

It was the first time that Robyn's extraordinary antics would cause such feelings. It wouldn't be the last.

PRESENT DAY

And so, getting a diagnosis for Robyn wasn't nearly as complicated for us as we know it is with many people. She was only 3 when we got a diagnosis of 'mild autism'. To be honest, they were probably hedging their bets with that use of 'mild'. At age 3, would you really be able to tell if someone had only mild autism? The only surprise about the diagnosis was that adjective and, as time went on, it was more and more clear that Robyn's autism was far from mild. Of course, now we are discouraged from using terms like 'mild' and 'severe' as they are not considered helpful, but we'll talk more about that later.

Liberty (we usually call her Libby) also got a diagnosis, and when it came it was more surprising. Libby's behaviour was certainly not typical, and there was clearly some developmental delay, but she seemed quite different to her sister. There were lots of theories amongst family and friends that Libby's progression was actually being hampered by her older sister. The example she had at home all the time was not an example that was going to lead to fast progress and high achievement. Libby would be OK, we reasoned, it's just that Robyn is slowing her development.

All parents of autistic children know that securing a diagnosis, getting that piece of paper to confirm what you already know as parents, is crucial in order to obtain the support that you need, and in order for your child to access the services necessary for them to progress. One of the services that we had access to once Robyn had been diagnosed was 'Sibs Group'. This was a playgroup held during school holidays at the local hospital for young siblings of autistic kids, to help them by giving them a break from some of the difficult times at home. George went to Sibs in his younger years, and Libby also went went along when she was old enough. And, rather oddly, this was actually how Libby was able to get an early diagnosis. When the carers at the group saw Libby's difficulties they were able to recognise them and put Libby forward for testing for autism.

Because she was so different from Robyn, I honestly thought, or hoped, that she wasn't autistic. I remember quite well reading the letter from the hospital that confirmed her diagnosis of autism. That was sobering. Robyn's diagnosis came as no surprise and was just confirmation of what we already knew; but this was different. Before this diagnosis, we had three children, one of whom was autistic. Now the autistic section of our children had a two thirds majority. When I was a kid I read a book about juggling, though I never actually learned to juggle. (This is the story of my life. I first had the idea of writing this book in about 2006; it's a miracle you're reading it even now.) In this book it explained that in terms of difficulty, juggling with 3 objects rated 6 out of 10, juggling with 4 objects was 8 out of 10, and juggling with 5 objects was 35 out of 10.

Adding one more autistic child to our family didn't mean our troubles had doubled. The lives of each member of our family had got considerably more than twice as hard.

FEARLESS - ESCAPES & OTHER DANGERS

BLOG POST FROM MARCH 11 2011 - FREEDOM

*S*ecurity measures in our home:

1 – Front and back door locks

2 – Window locks on all windows (always kept locked and keys hidden)

3 – Certain upstairs windows customised with restrictors so they can only open a maximum of two inches

4 – Key pad number locks on 8 internal doors

5 – Weighted fire door at foot of stairs

6 – 9 smoke alarms

7 – Alarms that are triggered by either front or back door opening

8 – Minimum six foot fence around all areas of garden, rising to eight feet in vulnerable places

9 – Bespoke wrought iron six foot garden gate with sheet metal reinforcements to prevent climbing

10 – Number coded box in which all keys are kept

11 – Infra-red beams placed along all rear fences and back gate. If the beams are breached, a message is sent to a pager to alert us as to where the breach is

The numbered security locks that are on every internal
door in our house

You may well reasonably ask, just who are these people? Is the area they live in really that rough? How paranoid about safety do you have to be to put such stringent security in place? Have they watched one too many episodes of Crimewatch (clearly these are the people that did have nightmares)? Or, most likely, you are already one step ahead of me. All of this security is not to keep people out of our house; it's to keep certain people in.

I told you last week about Robyn's first escape at the age of two. Since then, much of the energy that we have as relatives of Robyn has been spent on keeping her safe. Thankfully, Liberty likes being around the home and rarely shows a desire to escape, so it's just the one child we have to watch in this regard. But trust me on this; one Robyn is more than enough.

Robyn had a report written about her escaping, written by a social worker assessing our need for improved security. Rather brilliantly, she described Robyn as 'highly motivated' to escape as she found it 'extremely rewarding'. Add this to her total lack of fear, surprising upper body strength, natural agility and problem solving skills and you have a perfect escapologist storm brewing. So often we have caught her with one leg over the fence, about to break loose from her shackles and wreak havoc on the world. On such occasions we are able to pull her back to safety and whisper quiet prayers of gratitude that we have caught her in time. On other occasions, we are not nearly so lucky.

When Robyn was four, we moved from our 'two up two down' house in town to a bigger property in a much more rural area. This means that our house backs onto fields where the local farmer's cows graze. As stated previously, Robyn is fearless. Let me explain what I mean by that. Imagine you or I were standing on the flat roof of a 500 foot building and another 500 foot building was just a yard or two away. If someone dared us to jump across the gap, we would most likely refuse. Despite the fact that those of us who are sufficiently youthful know we could make the jump, perhaps quite easily, the possible consequences of us failing in some way gives us a healthy sense of fear that prevents us from doing such things. Now, Robyn isn't stupid; she knows falling 500 feet isn't a good thing. But if she wanted to cross that gap and was confident she could make it, she would. The only consideration she has when attempting something dangerous is this; do I have the skills to do it?

As far as Robyn is concerned, consequences are for wimps. So when she escapes into the farmer's field, she happily runs past the young bulls grazing there without any fear. The only thing on her mind is the nearby farmer's barn where she can wallow thigh deep in cow poo. However, unlike Robyn, I possess a regular amount of fear and judgement, and running past such animals is not top of my 'things to do before I die' list. Mainly because I fear it will be the very last thing I accomplish before I do actually die. I vividly recall the time we discovered how aggressive these young creatures can be. My son George was given a leg up over the fence to bring Robyn safely back after we had seen her mid-escape, so he went in the field with the young 'cows'; how was I to know they were bulls? These rather large and imposing beasts started charging at George and Robyn preventing their safe return. It all turned out fine in the end, but I didn't send George in with the cows after that!

When Robyn does escape it can be very stressful for everyone present, as I'm sure you can imagine. The one positive aspect of this anxiety is that Liberty picks up on it, and she doesn't like it. So, bizarrely, one of our most successful security measures to keep our autistic daughter safe is actually our other autistic daughter. Despite being younger and smaller, Libby is bossier and pushier than Robyn, and, due to her placid nature, Robyn allows Libby to boss her about. I don't usually like this aspect of Liberty's nature, but when I look into the garden and see her dragging Robyn down from an 8 foot fence whilst telling her off, I am rather grateful for Libby's assertiveness.

There are lots of less funny stories I could tell you about our 'highly motivated' escapee, and I'm sure you'll hear them in time. But today, I'm just going to admire the determination and phys-ical and mental strength Robyn shows to overcome any and all obstacles we place in her path. Whatever security we put in place, she seems to find a way around it. When I first suggested Robyn could have a security chip implanted in her leg so we could trace her movements, Social Services just laughed. Except I wasn't joking, and after a while neither were they; they began to look into whether or not it was possible. So maybe it won't be too long before they take my best idea seriously, the one that would really solve the problem: a 50 foot gun tower built in our back garden, manned 24 hours a day by a crack team of prison guards armed with guns and tranquilliser darts. Honestly, I think it's the only way we'll ever stop her.

BLOG POST FROM APRIL 28 2011 - THE SWEET ESCAPE

It's the early evening. Dinner has been served and Robyn and Liberty have made an almighty mess with an unfeasibly large amount of curry. George has settled into a night of Blackberry messaging, pointless internet game playing and watching

Scrubs on the TV in the playroom. Karen and I are trying to watch one of our television shows that we've recorded for when we get a few minutes peace: It might be *Mad Men*, *Lie To Me*, *The Good Wife* or any of those other dramas that the Americans have suddenly got awfully good at making. And our daughters? They'll be in the lounge on various computer and iPad type machines. Hopefully. And if we're not 100% sure where they are and we can't hear them, well, that's when the trouble starts. That's when we get a knock on the door from one of the kids playing in the street, and those door knocks are never good.

I remember the first time it happened. It was a Monday night and we had obviously not kept a sharp enough eye on Robyn. There was a knock at the door from a neighbour; 'Did you know your daughter's on the roof?' 'Why, yes we did', we replied, 'but we figured we'd just let her hang out up there for a while to entertain you all.'

If the prospect of a 7 year-old child on the roof of a house doesn't fill you with some sort of horror, then go outside right now and take a look at your roof. We live in a fairly standard British two storey house, not like lots of American homes where there is a basement and one storey above ground. So go outside and imagine seeing your special needs kid sitting on the chimney stack two storeys up, enjoying the view as if it's the most natural activity in the world. It's higher than you think.

You see, Robyn likes heights and always has done. When we visit somewhere, she'll often look for the highest point in the room to make herself comfortable, even if that's on the top of a cupboard. At our old house we used to have one of those old style gas cookers with the grill at the top around eye level which is very handy for keeping an eye on your toast or fish fingers. It was also a great place for Robyn to hang out, sitting on top of the grill, eating Monster Munch, swinging her feet above the burning gas hobs. We did used to quickly get her down from *there, in case you were wondering, but Robyn was never too concerned about the danger.*

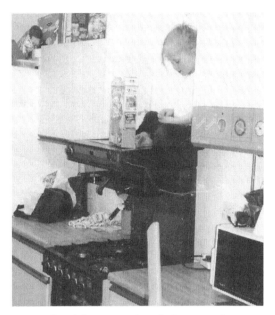

Robyn chilling out on the grill of our gas cooker

So, what do you do when your daughter is 40 feet up on a roof? What do you do when she climbs to the apex of the roof and then starts sliding down the entire roof to the guttering like it's some majorly awesome slide? What do you do when she is on the roof and you live at the end of a four house terrace, so she walks all the way along the roof apex from your house all the way up to the roof of No.42? The first thing you do is ignore all the disapproving comments about your parenting skills from the rapidly gathering crowd of people in the street, who have decided that an autistic kid risking life and limb on the roof is way more entertaining than that night's Coronation Street. And, of course, you call the fire brigade. The first time it happened, they got a long ladder out, climbed up and tried to coax her down. Funnily enough, she wasn't very interested in coming down for the nice fireman; she was having a great time! So I had to climb up the ladder with the fireman and see if she was more likely to come down if Daddy asked nicely. Thankfully, she did.

Obviously, we were a lot more vigilant after that. The scariest part was how she had got up there; a manoeuvre that was quite astonishing. She had got onto the roof by opening an upstairs window and using the open window frame itself as an aide to get onto the roof. And think about it, roofs have overhanging eves so you've got to go backwards in order to go up. Anyway, a while later they were building our house extension, so the back of the house had scaffolding about it all the way up to the roof, and she got up again.

This time it was the 23rd December and we were awaiting our friends Kate & Spike who were coming over for our annual pre-Christmas dinner. Someone must have left the patio door at the back of the house unlocked, and I'd left the room for two minutes. And two minutes is all Robyn needs. When I realised she'd gone I searched everywhere in the garden for her, but after a minute or two I had to force myself to look up. And there she was. Sitting on the chimney stack, swinging her bare feet back and forth, squealing with excitement and contentment, not scared or worried in the least. I had to scale the scaffolding and stand near the roof, making sure she stayed where she was. The chimney may not be the safest place to be, but it was much safer for her to stay there than indulge in the roof top slide shenanigans she'd gone for last time.

To make things worse, this had happened on my watch. Again. Karen was out and returned to find a fire engine and another huge crowd outside the house. It may have been Christmas, but there still wasn't anything good enough on TV to compete with the spectacle of Robyn on the roof, live and without a net! This time the fire brigade unleashed the cherry picker to rescue her. This was no doubt the safest way of bringing Robyn down to earth, but I don't think it exactly discouraged her from trying to get up there again. A cherry picker? What larks! When she came down she was completely untraumatised (unlike her parents) and, other than being a bit cold, was completely well and utterly oblivious to all the fuss she had caused.

The famous photo of Robyn sitting on the chimney pot

There was one more occasion when she managed to return to her most exciting hangout. This time I don't know all the details because I wasn't there (and is it wrong of me to be secretly pleased that something this awful happened to my wife as well, just to prove that it wasn't just me who's useless?) I returned home from some duties I'd been carrying out at church to find a fire engine, ambulance and police car outside our house. I don't think I'm exaggerating when I say that that's never a good sign, is it? Robyn had escaped onto the roof whilst Karen was ironing. George and Karen had been dealing with that situation, so that left Libby unattended for a few minutes, and she decided this was a good opportunity to play with a red hot iron. Someone from the fire crew had called an ambulance to deal with Liberty's burn (though it turned out not to be very serious). I'm not sure why the police turned up; possibly they felt a bit left out or something and wanted to get in on all the action.

And that is the story of Robyn and the roof. It hasn't happened for a few years now, but we still get urgent knocks on the door from time to time from the local kids. They've come to tell us that George has left his window and bedroom door unlocked and Robyn is hanging out of the window, negotiating the route to a return to the scene of her greatest triumphs.

PRESENT DAY

Ten years on, the good news is that, within a few years, Robyn gave up on the escaping. We never have to worry about her running off or escaping to the roof these days. Grown up Robyn still likes a thrill; she loves her theme park rides and, even when doing something as mundane as driving around in the car, she loves to hang out of the window with the wind in her face, giggling to herself. But her escaping days are over.

How Robyn likes to travel in the car

You might be wondering how that happened. Well, ever heard the analogy of the fleas in the jar? You probably have. If you put a flea in a jar, it will jump out. If you put a lid on the jar, they will continue trying to escape for a while but, eventually, they realise they can't escape and stop trying, even if the lid is removed. They have 'learned' they can't escape, even if they actually could. And that's what happened to Robyn. The wonderfully over the top infra red beams placed all around the garden perimeter, like something out of Mission: Impossible, were the real clincher. As I explained, when the beams were tripped by our lovely escapee on her way over the fence, a pager in the house would bleep to let us know, and even send us a message to let us know which part of the garden fence she was clambering over. Obviously, Robyn had no understanding of how we now seemed to always know when she was making a run for it. All she knew was that, suddenly, there was no point in trying anymore. Repeated failure meant that, eventually, she just stopped trying, which was a massive relief to all of us.

The infra red sensors are still out there on the garden perimeter, gathering dust and cobwebs now, but they did their job, and they serve as a testament to tough times gone by. Sometimes, during a family event at our home when we are out in the garden, Robyn's younger cousins will notice the sensors and ask what they are. When I explain that they are infra red sensors and why we had them installed, they think I'm joking. In fairness, that does sound like the kind of silly response that uncles make to ordinary questions, so their parents have to explain that Uncle Barn isn't kidding about the garden security. There really was a time when Robyn's escapology was such a risk that our garden was given the kind of security system usually afforded to bank vaults.

Becoming overgrown with leaves now, but the small black box
(centre-right) is one of the infrared sensors still on the fences in our
back garden

BLOG POST FROM APRIL 30 2011 - WE DIDN'T START THE FIRE

Extraordinary Facts About Robyn No.1 – Robyn has never broken a bone, had stitches, suffered a serious burn or had any need to attend the Accident & Emergency room of the hospital. When you consider the peril she puts herself in daily, this is an extraordinary fact indeed.

Liberty has had a couple of minor things patched up, but no stitches or broken bones. When I was their age, my Mum was on first name terms with the nurses in the Accident & Emergency department. I have a rather cool looking scar in the shape of a cross on the underside of my chin. I didn't know it was there until I was 10, and when I asked my Mum how I did it, she tells me she can't remember. We injured ourselves so often it's all just a blur to her. My Mum is a very capable parent, so given how many injuries we had, and how few the girls have had, it's pretty aston-ishing. Libby has burned herself on an iron, though it wasn't much to shout about, but the fact that she has never burned herself with fire (or burned our home to the ground) is more remarkable yet.

Libby enjoying the firepit in our garden. She still loves fire...

Perhaps it all started with birthday candles. Libby and Robyn both enjoy the blowing out of the candles at people's birthday parties and, at most birthday parties that we attend, we know the hosts sufficiently well that they agree to relight the candles and have a second rendition of the traditional birthday tune so the girls can have a go at blowing out the candles as well. And, in all fairness, if an activity such as this is so much fun for them, why would they keep it just for birthdays?

It doesn't seem to matter where we hide the matches, Liberty will eventually find them. Then she will sit down somewhere quiet, lighting matches and blowing them out. If she can find some candles knocking about the place, she'll light those as well;

light them up, blow them out, set off one of our dozens of smoke alarms, annoy the neighbours, happy as the day is long.

Libby is so attracted to fire that she likes to watch scenes from films with fire in just to watch the fire burn. I recall a scene from Disney's The Hunchback of Notre Dame where Quasimodo swung a lit torch around at someone that we had to watch several hundred times in succession. There's a scene in another film where a character shouts, 'Fire! Fire!', which Libby likes to copy by shouting sometimes. One Saturday morning, Karen and I were attempting something of a lie-in, when Liberty burst into our room to wake us, shouting, 'Fire! Fire!' We did what any sensible parent would do in such circumstances and told her to be quiet and go and watch her film. A minute or two later, when the smoke alarms started screaming, we realised that she wasn't just quoting a film this time; she was trying to alert us to the fact that she had actually set the house on fire. It was only then that we responded and ran downstairs and found she'd got a big candle out of a cupboard, lit it, and then fuelled the fire with ripped up pieces of cardboard. It had got a bit out of control, but there wasn't too much damage to the furniture! An average Saturday morning in our house.

Robyn also likes to indulge in heat related antics, but more to do with the oven. We don't have a gas supply in our village, so we have to have an electric cooker. The hobs are those glowing red ones under a big piece of glass. One of Robyn's favourite tricks from days gone by was to switch the hobs on and then stand on them in her rubber soled shoes. The idea of her game was to let her shoes heat up so they started to melt and become 'tacky', then she would lift her feet up and down, stretching the melted rubber so it looked like mozzarella on a slice of pizza when you move it from the rest of the pizza. Obviously, she couldn't get away with this for too long as the smell of burning rubber wafting through the house was a dead giveaway, but we *lost a fair number of pairs of shoes due to this ridiculously dangerous game.*

Thinking about the oven has reminded me of another story about Libby. The girls don't indulge in as much weird and wonderful behaviour as they used to, but there are times when they do things that make you think they are deliberately being obtuse. It's as if, every now and again, they want to remind you that they're properly autistic and indulge in utterly bizarre behaviour just to keep you on your toes. Thankfully, the girls also tend to keep their clothes on a little more these days which, given that they are now 13 and 10, is a huge relief. But when they were younger they would whip their clothes off at the drop of a hat, which I gather is quite common in autistic kids. They must like the wind whistling around them or something.

Anyway, the story it reminded me of was when I walked into the kitchen a few years ago and found Liberty lying naked in front of the oven. Not just naked, though. She had been into the cupboards and dug out a bottle of vegetable oil, in which she had slathered herself from head to toe whilst writhing around the kitchen floor. With my empathetic autistic head on, I can under-stand this; it's all about the sensory experience of your slippery skin on the polished floor. But then she went back to the cupboard and retrieved a large container of oregano in which she then rolled herself, all the oregano sticking to both her body and the floor. Having to walk in to the kitchen to find a naked child, covered in oil and oregano lying in front of the oven, basted like a chicken, a situation that was going to take a fair amount of cleaning (both floor and child), well, the thought did occur to me to put the oven on a medium heat, open the door and just chuck her in. Tempting. But the fact that I am writing this from my living room rather than a prison cell let's you know that I resisted…

PRESENT DAY

When you hear about the dangers in which the girls involved themselves in our kitchen, you might wonder why we let them in there at all. After all, this is a house with infra red beams around the garden, why not a lock on the kitchen door?

The custom built kitchen door, complete with
number secutity lock

The problem was that there was no kitchen door. The kitchen was part of an extension that had been built in the past, and the builders had elected just to put a large archway into the kitchen that was far too big for a regular door. When the council started to realise the extent of the problems we were having with Robyn and Libby and started to think a little outside the box to help us, they got someone in to construct a kitchen door. It had to be completely bespoke due to its large size and arch shape, but we do now have a kitchen door with a number lock, which has helped keep the girls' kitchen based shenanigans to a minimum ever since. It's also a bit of a feature; like something out of Lord of the Rings. Cool.

BLOG POST FROM JULY 2 2011 - I NEED A DOCTOR

This morning I had to give out letters to some of the kids in my class of 12-13 year olds, encouraging them to get their MMR jab. There is a legacy from the scare over the MMR jab which jeopardises the general immunity of kids in this country from measles, mumps and rubella. You may recall a few years back that a doctor alleged there was a link between the MMR vaccination and autism. Right when the hoo-ha about all this kicked off we were just discovering that Robyn was autistic, so it concerned us more than most. Our experience with the MMR jab is different to most families, and it goes a little something like this:

George: Received the MMR jab. Not autistic.

Robyn: Received the MMR jab. Autistic.

Liberty: Did not receive MMR jab. Autistic.

(NB Libby did get the jab later.)

If I was a scientist, I could probably draw conclusions from this to support a theory, mainly because scientists can always find evidence to support a theory if you pay them enough. Anybody else will declare that these facts tell us exactly nothing about the situation. We didn't let Libby have the jab initially because the hysteria about the MMR was at its height and we already had one autistic kid. I think most people could understand our reticence. Most people doesn't include our family doctor at the time, who made my wife feel stupid for being concerned about a widely reported story that had direct relevance to our family, and told us we should get Liberty jabbed straight away. I think part of the reason we didn't was just to spite the doctor. Thank goodness he retired soon after.

Our dealings with doctors have not all been negative, however. We have encountered and been treated by some top guys and gals from the medical profession over the years. Our dentist, Gilly, for example, is terrific with the girls; her excellent 'bedside manner' with our children means we'd never change our dentist. In recent years, Robyn has become very compliant and co-operative in these types of situations. She enjoys having a ride up and down on the dentist chair, and seems to get a kick out of donning the health & safety shades they insist you wear these days. We've never been daring enough to actually give her any proper treatment, so we were quite happy for a couple of her milk teeth to go a bit manky, but now that she is happy (well, willing, at least) to have her teeth brushed at home and checked by the dentist, her adult teeth are in much better shape.

Libby quite enjoys a trip to the dentist, too, as long as you don't actually try to do any of that silly nonsense where you put her in the chair to have her teeth checked. She likes running around the place, putting on the glasses, blowing up the rubber gloves, swigging the mouthwash, playing with the dentist's drill, pinching a few stickers and otherwise playing merry hell, but she's not so keen on all that teeth prodding that these dentist types seem to go in for. We've always been slightly disappointed with this because, as you may know, the dentist is a crucial setting in top Disney/Pixar movie 'Finding Nemo'. In fact, there are several scenes in the film that Libby likes to act out, and she is obsessed with anyone she meets who wears braces on their teeth, insisting on constantly looking in their mouth and calling them 'Darla' (a dentally challenged character who we meet in the film), but she's not digging the entire proper dentist experience, per se.

However, the last time we went to the dentists there was a breakthrough. And in typical Libby/Robyn style, it wasn't a minor one. Libby went from refusing to go anywhere near the dentist chair, to a perfect full dental check, including a bit of a polish on her teeth. Do not think we've cracked it; it's quite likely she'll absolutely refuse to play ball next time.

(NB Libby has been fine at the dentist ever since).

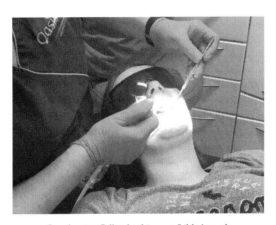

Our dentist, Gilly, checking out Libby's teeth

ROBYN HAS ALWAYS HAD PROBLEMS WITH HER EARS AND HAS HAD TO have grommets and exploratory surgery on a few occasions. Her inability to communicate means that she has to be put to sleep to have tests done to determine her hearing capability; if she can't tell us when she is hurt or what she wants for dinner, she's hardly going to be able to tell us exactly which sounds she can hear. The whole process of putting Robyn to sleep and waking her up for these minor operations can be difficult and stressful, so with her last operation occurring during the summer holiday,

Karen asked me to take Robyn on this occasion. It's not just a tough situation for Robyn; Karen finds the whole procedure very upsetting.

When you work and your wife is a stay-at-home mum, you quite often miss out on lots of the day-to-day responsibilities of being a parent. So I quite enjoyed the opportunity to step up and be the hands-on parent on a big occasion like this. It wasn't an overnight stay, just an hour or two for some tests, then the operation, wake up, make sure she's all OK and then go home.

We got to the hospital and said goodbye to Karen and then I got Robyn into her pyjamas and dealt with the tests whilst Robyn watched the iPad. The iPad had only just come out and was still quite a novelty for everyone who saw it, but it was a real godsend in the hospital as Robyn had a good sized extremely portable screen to watch her movies on wherever we took her, which helped keep her calm. When we went down to the oper- ating theatre (she loved the ride down on the bed!) I sat on the bed and held her in my arms whilst we tried to get the anaes- thetising mask onto her face to get her to sleep. As we were sitting there, I chatted to the doctor about Robyn:

Doctor: So at what age did she get her diagnosis of autism?

Me: We knew there was a problem quite early on, but she was three when we got an initial diagnosis.

Doctor: And what sort of problems do you usually have with her ears?

Me: They're very waxy and runny and she quite often gets earache which then…

Doctor: Oooh, is that an iPad?

Me: Er, yeah, yeah it is.

Doctor: Are they as good as people are saying?

Me: Yeah, er, it's great.

Doctor: The screen resolution's amazing isn't it?

Me: Yeah, er, listen Doc, we're about to cut my daughters

head open. The iPad is awesome, absolutely, but can we not, you know, focus on the job in hand for a minute?

OK, I didn't actually say that last bit, but I did think it. And as I spoke words of reassurance to Robyn, we managed to get the mask onto her face for sufficient time to get her to sleep. Once she was gone I had that unexplainably heartbreaking moment of leaving your child in an operating theatre, unconscious and help-less. You know everything will be fine, but what can you do? You're a dad. It's your job to worry about your kids. I kissed her sleeping face and left her in the hands of her capable but slightly distracted doctor. I took the iPad with me, otherwise the doctor wouldn't have got anything done. Besides, I needed it to read that day's edition of The Times while I was waiting.

Robyn really didn't enjoy waking up from the anaesthetic. I think most people feel groggy and miserable when waking up after an operation, but what you always have to take into account with Robyn is that she doesn't know what's going on. She has no understanding of what's just happened, why she feels off colour and, frankly, why the hell you've just woken her up when she was having a perfectly good sleep. It took a long time to calm her down. I tried all kinds of things: the iPad, rides in a wheelchair, going for a walk with her on my shoulders, Pepsi… nothing was stopping her from crying. But the nurses wanted to see she had calmed down and preferably had something to eat before they allowed us to go home.

After more than an hour of Robyn's constant tears, I had an idea. Hand in hand, we went for a walk down to the shop in the hospital to see if there was anything I could tempt her with. Thankfully, they had a little ice cream freezer that stocked Magnums (a chocolate covered ice cream). I managed to stop her from eating it until we got back to the ward so the nurses could watch her crack the chocolate, peel it off the Magnum, scoff it, and then chuck the ice cream in the bin. Well, if they didn't know she was autistic before…

3

THIS IS ME TRYING -
COMMUNICATION
PRESENT DAY

ere's a question. And, I suppose, depending on when you're reading this and how up to date your knowledge is, there could be a variety of answers. What do you call a person who has autism? When our girls were diagnosed, back in the early 2000s, you simply said that a person who had autism was 'autistic', and so that's what we did. Then, a few years down the line, I read that calling someone 'autistic' was poor form; 'autistic' suggested that was the only facet to their being. Instead, you should say that the person 'has autism', which instead suggests that this is only one part of who they are.

I'll be honest, I'm not that bothered about these things. This is possibly because of the severity of our girls' autism, if you'll allow me to say that. They don't understand that they even have autism, so how we describe them in this regard is of literally no interest to them. But I understand that many people with autism are very aware of the condition they have, so, because I'm a caring kind of fella, I started trying to say 'has autism' rather than 'autistic'. Then, around 2020, I started reading people with autism saying, 'Don't say I have autism, I'm autistic.' What? I've only just got used to saying 'has autism'! Don't move the goal-posts again!

Apparently, according to the Centre for Autism Research, the majority of adults with autism prefer the term autistic, although professionals prefer 'has autism'. Well, given a choice between pleasing those who actually have the condition and stuffy old medical professionals, I'll definitely give my thumbs up to the autistic guys and gals out there. But this shows that even those within the autistic community are fairly divided on exactly what language to use. And I spent the best part of twenty years training myself to say 'has autism' or 'with autism' instead of 'autistic', and now the word autistic actually sounds dated and 'wrong' in my mind.

It's a bit like the word 'queer' when used in the LGBTQ sense. The word 'queer' certainly got used to describe gay people when I was growing up, but it was always in a pejorative way. For many of us, hearing the term used so openly in a positive way when talking about gay people is still a bit jarring. OK, just to be clear, I wouldn't quite equate using 'autistic' to describe people with autism as the same as people now saying 'queer' when describing gay people, but if you can understand how the change seems a little odd and disconcerting, that's how this is for me. Going back to 'autistic' feels difficult.

Then, in a society completely obsessed with labelling everyone and everything, all the labels within the autistic spectrum began to change. The school I taught at from 1999 was referred to as an 'Asperger's Base', which is to say, it was the high school in the area where kids who had Asperger's Syndrome came to be educated. But then the powers that be (who actually makes these decisions?), decided that we shouldn't refer to Asperger's anymore. We just talked about ASD. Everyone who had autism, whatever type, just had autism. They were 'on the spectrum'. Then, in a further development, it was decided that it also wasn't helpful to try to say where someone was on the spectrum.

The National Autistic Society say I shouldn't refer to severe or mild autism, and I kind of get why that is, but if I tell someone that my daughters have autism, what do they imagine? They probably imagine someone they know who has autism and imagine Robyn and Libby are like that. But, if the person they're imagining is someone who is able to mostly cope with everyday life, maybe with just a little support, they have imagined my daughters in a way that isn't even remotely accurate.

Can I say high or low functioning, then, to give the person I'm talking to a bit of a heads up as to the situation we're talking about? Nope. The PC gods have given that the thumbs down, too. And I do get why. I understand that in some circumstances it can be demeaning and reductive to talk about people in that way. But, as I've already said, my daughters don't even know the word 'autism'. It makes absolutely no difference to them how they're described. Literally none. And when I'm spending half my evening cleaning poo off the walls, or being beaten black and blue, you'll forgive me for not spending the other half of my evening reading about what changes have been made this week about what I can and can't say about my daughters who barely understand a word I'm saying to begin with.

And for exactly how long will the current trends of describing autism last? I'll just get used to making whatever changes to my language that I need to make, and then somebody, somewhere, will decide there's a new term to use, or something else I can't say. And if you think the language won't change, you're wrong. People actually in the community can't even agree among themselves about exactly what to say, so you can guarantee that we'll be told, sooner or later, that the language we've been using will no longer be fit for purpose. And it still won't actually make any difference to the quality of Robyn or Liberty's life, and it won't give us as parents any extra strength to deal with the difficulties that their challenges have also brought to us. I'm not saying that other people can't be concerned about the language used around autism. Call it what you want. I'm just saying that I've got bigger fish to fry.

BLOG POST FROM MARCH 17 2011 - EVERYTHING SHE WANTS

Liberty really only speaks in what speech therapists call 'echolalia'. Parrot-like, she can repeat everything she hears, though she often has very little clue of what she is saying. However, Libby's ability to speak means that, over a certain length of time, she has come to understand some words sufficiently to communicate her basic needs to us: 'rice', 'popcorn', 'dinner', 'drinking' and, of course, the names of many, many films that she likes to watch. Robyn cannot do any of these things. Robyn doesn't say a word. And yet, when the Rolling Stones claimed you can't always get what you want, they clearly hadn't met Robyn.

Liberty talks constantly, but very little of what she says actually makes much sense. Most of her speech is quoting large chunks of her favourite films, not always entirely coherently. Sometimes, it's easy to recognise what she is saying as we have heard that scene many times before. Both girls like to watch certain sections of a film repeatedly. When people visit our house and the girls are playing the same ten second sequence of a movie over and over again, they look at us and ask incredulously, 'Doesn't that drive you completely nuts?' What they actually mean is, 'That is driving me completely nuts'. The answer to their original question is, 'Not really'. Karen, George and I don't really hear it anymore; we've just learned to tune it out.

Anyway, the point is, we've come to understand that most of what Liberty is saying doesn't really mean much; she just likes the sound of it. When Libby runs around the house shouting in an American accent, 'You know, I'm really, really busy!', we know she's just quoting from Coraline (her current favourite film). She often speaks in an American accent much of the time, and why shouldn't she? She doesn't understand most of what she says, she just copies it exactly as she hears it; to her they are just sounds. The people in films speak like that, and she's just copying them. In fact, Libby can go one better than that. She likes to find clips on YouTube that are related to her favourite films and, YouTube being an international website, some of the things she watches are in foreign languages. But hey, if none of the words you hear make any sense to you to begin with, why not watch something in a foreign language if it looks and sounds good? And if you speak in echolalia, surely it doesn't make any difference to you what language you are copying? To you, they're all just sounds. So, whilst my youngest only speaks a handful of words with genuine meaning, she can happily run about the place seemingly speaking fluent Japanese. True story.

George has taught Libby a short conversation so he can feel like he is actually communicating with his little sister. It goes like this:

George: Hello, Libby
Libby: Hello, George
George: Are you OK?
Libby: I'm OK.

It's a script that George has painstakingly taught to Liberty, but sadly, it doesn't mean much to her, other than being a bit of a fun game. She also likes her mum and me to act out scenes from films with her. There are lots of scenes in Coraline where the title character speaks with her parents and Libby likes to come and act them out with us. Bit by bit we have learned our parts, and although we know it isn't a real conversation, it is nice to actually interact with her. What is less good is that she also likes to make buttons out of paper and glue them to our eyes like Coraline's 'other' mother and father in the film. It may supposed to be for kids, but Coraline is one creepy film.

Given Liberty's constant film quoting in an array of languages, it is perhaps something of a blessing that Robyn doesn't speak. That isn't to say she doesn't make noise. She likes to sing, though it's rarely a recognisable melody. She will also make more aggressive noises when she is frustrated, and those familiar with autistic children will have some idea of what they sound like. My favourite sound she makes is her laughter, which fortunately we hear quite frequently. She laughs when she is tickled, she laughs when you play 'rough & tumble' with her, but mostly she just laughs when something strikes her as funny. Unfortunately, there is not usually a noticeable trigger for her amusement, so it's rare that we get to share the joke, but it's always nice to see her happy, even if she seems to be laughing at nothing. In school, Robyn uses Makaton sign language and pictures to communicate. However, we have tried these systems at home and she's not having any of it. School is school and home is home and never the twain shall meet, as far as Robyn is concerned.

So Robyn's most effective way of communicating at home is through the bringing of objects and the dragging of people. If she wants to watch a movie, she brings me the remote. If she wants some curry, she brings me a bowl and spoon. If she wants to get through a locked door, she drags me to it and puts my hand on the handle. If she wants to go outside, she puts her coat and shoes on and stands in front of me expectantly. If Libby has taken Robyn's iPad and she wants it back, she comes and takes my laptop that I'm using (she knows that I will then be sufficiently motivated to go and get the iPad back off Libby for her). Pictures and actions are used to communicate at school, at home she just drags us to different places. Whatever works, kid.

She may not be able to speak but, as Wham! would have it,

Robyn always finds a way to get everything she wants.

PRESENT DAY

When Libby watches YouTube she can watch what she wants and she has her headphones on, so we can't always supervise properly. She watches some odd stuff: the trailer to a horror film called The Ruins which she always likes to watch in Spanish, and some bizarre Disney Princess stuff, including one clip where someone has animated them in the aftermath of a car crash (what kind of sicko makes this stuff?) Of course, she can also hear language that isn't great for her to copy, which we've had to keenly discourage. Being religious types, it has also taken us lots of training to get her not to copy the full 'OMG' phrase that she hears, so she now always says 'Oh my gosh' instead, which we are pleased with. She has also recently started singing the children's song 'I Am A Child of God' which is lovely to hear. However, applying the same logic we have taught her, she insists on singing 'I Am A Child of Gosh'.

Libby's speech has come on a lot over the last ten years. It's still very limited, but she can have simple conversations now. One of her favourite things to explain to you is when she'll be getting her favourite fast food. 'KFC, 4 pieces of chicken - 2 more sleeps. McDonald's, 3 cheeseburgers, chips, Coca-cola drink - 6 more sleeps. Pizza Hut, salami pizza - 12 more sleeps.' It's not often she gets three lots of her favourites in twelve days, but that's the kind of thing she would say if she did. There is a lot that's repetitious about the things she says, but she definitely understands a lot of what she says to us now. That's quite a bit of progress.

Libby will also adapt film quotes to her conversational needs. If you offer her something she doesn't want, or suggest an activity she doesn't want to do, she will often reply, quite tersely, 'No, thank you!' You might think this is being polite, and I suppose it is, but she's actually just quoting Belle in Beauty and the Beast when Beast invites her to dinner. Other quotes she's used in conversation have included telling us to get out of her room with a quote from The Prince of Egypt ('You have my permission to go. Leave me!'), or when she burps or breaks wind we get an appropriate quote from Shrek 2 ('Better out than in, that's what I always say, right Fiona?'). Another Shrek 2 favourite that can really get across her negative reaction to something is to copy the tone of Jennifer Saunders' Fairy Godmother by shouting, 'No! No! No! No! No!' A few years back, when she wanted something from her Dad, she would chase me around shouting, 'Father! Father!' which was from Disney's Pinocchio. Now, when speaking to me, she borrows a quote from Macaulay Culkin (one of her favourites because of Home Alone) from the start of Michael Jackson's 'Black Or White' video, saying, in a slightly whiny, exasperated way, 'But, Daaaad...'. I preferred the Pinocchio one.

She still likes to randomly quote films to herself at great length, but I'm grateful for that. You see, Liberty and I have had quite a few years now where we've not been close at all. It wasn't really anyone's fault, it was just the way it panned out. When you've got two autistic children and two parents, then each of you obviously take one kid each whenever you go somewhere. And, for whatever reason, when we were out and about, Libby tended to grab Mum's hand. After a while, Libby would only grab Mum's hand, and Dad became someone who was around, who could still be relied upon to get her food and fix her devices, but not someone she had any affection for. I'm not going to lie, it's been tough to take at times. I would go out of my way to do things for her that I knew she would love, buy her things that I knew she really wanted, and it would always be greeted with indifference. If her mum was there, she would chide

Libby for being ungrateful with a 'What do you say to Daddy?' And Libby would say 'Thank you', and lean her forehead forward to graciously allow me to kiss her on the head. But I was a servant to Libby, and not much else, for a fair few years.

I'm a pretty good servant, though, and, over time, I was able to provide her with services that even her beloved Mum couldn't. For a start, as I intimated, Dad is the one who knows all about the electronics that she depends on. If anything goes wrong with her desktop computer, iPad, TV channels, Wifi, logins to websites, the printer, whatever, Libby knows that many of life's problems will be fixed by Mum but, in our house, at least, this is Dad territory. (Just as an aside, Karen does all the DIY, fixes cars and other things, and I'm entirely happy with the cooking and cleaning; there aren't too many gender stereotypes in our marriage, but I am a bit geeky and techy and Karen is happy to leave that stuff to me).

Then, as she's got older, Libby's love of movies has led to her to not just enjoying the films themselves, but also finding out about the people who made them. She likes to watch lots of 'making of' videos on YouTube and knows the names of all the actors in her favourite films. She has an amazing knowledge of the people who have worked on those movies and surprises us by knowing things we didn't have a clue about. We were watching The Good Wife one night when Libby walked in, pointed at the screen and shouted, 'Christine Baranski!' I checked online and, sure enough, the actress on screen was Christine Baranski. Of course, Libby knew her as Martha May from The Grinch, but it showed she could recognise actors and understands the concept of how actors are different to characters. And that's another area where Dad's geekiness helps. Sometimes she wants to know the name of an actor that she hasn't come across before, and Dad will be the one to help, either through his own pretty decent knowledge of movies or with a little help from my IMDb app.

For a long time, Libby would come to her Mum and demand for her to act out this long piece she had put together with scenes from 101 Dalmatians, Cinderella, Maleficent and The Magic Roundabout. Every time Karen visited her at her residence they would have to spend about ten minutes acting it out together. She's stopped doing it now, but she has started doing two scenes with Dad. One from Shrek, with Lord Farquaard torturing the Gingerbread Man ('Do you know the Muffin Man?'), and one from The Goonies where Chunk tells the story about making everyone throw up in the movie theatre ('But the worst thing I ever did…'). I think it's a combination of these things, and maybe Libby moving out and appreciating home more, that have brought us a little closer. Hugs for Dad are no longer completely out of the ordinary, and she will happily sit with me and 'talk' about films. I will give her the name of an actor and she will tell me what film she knows them from. Maybe it's not much, but it's a lot more attention than I am used to, and I'm grateful for what I get.

Libby and me watching 'The Ant Bully' together

In addition to improvements in her speech, Libby has developed some reading and writing skills. When I say reading, the truth is, what she does is recognises words. But isn't that what we all do most of the time? We're not sounding out words unless it's a word we're unfamiliar with, we just recognise the shape of the word, so we know what it says. Libby started out by being able to read the titles of films, but then added the names of characters and actors and then a few other bits and pieces. She can spell them all correctly, too, although, it's entirely logical that she would spell those words correctly because she isn't relying on a logic of what letters sound like; most of the time she doesn't understand how letters correspond to sounds. What she is doing is memorising a picture. When you and I struggle to spell a word, we do our best to use the letters that sound like they might be in the word. Libby just sees a picture of the word in her head and reproduces it, either with a pen or on a computer keyboard. So she always spells words right, even if it's a difficult spelling because, to her, there are no difficult spellings. Libby doesn't umm and ahh about I before E, or have to remember complex mnemonics. She either remembers the picture of the word, or she doesn't. And if she does, she'll spell it right.

Because Liberty decided not to have too much to do with me for most of her teenage years, it was Karen who naturally had considerably more input into her life than me. But, as I've said before, I continued trying to help make a difference in her life, and I never tired of coming up with little ideas that I hoped would help her. And one day, I came up with a corker that ended up being a real game changer.

My Mum always tells me, so I assume it's true, that one of the last things that falls into place for small children is a genuine perception of time. If you tell a little kid that their birthday is in three months, what does that even mean to them? You may as well have said it was eight years away. And this was the problem we had with Libby. Going into her mid-teens, Libby understood the idea of a day pretty well; like a lot of small children do, she called them 'sleeps'. So, in the short term, that was an effective way to measure time. That's where the whole 'KFC, 3 pieces of chicken, 2 more sleeps!' works really well. But then Libby comes downstairs one day and says, 'Christmas? Yes?' and it's still the middle of summer. How are we going to explain this?

Libby was so used to getting her own way and bargaining for what she wanted that she thought she could now even change the Gregorian calendar. If she asked for Christmas right now, surely we should be able to make it happen? The only response we had for her in those circumstances was to pull a sad face and say, 'Lots of sleeps, Libby. Still lots of sleeps until Christmas', and that didn't really make the situation any clearer for her.

Then I had an idea. One of those, 'it probably won't work, but it's worth a shot', kind of things. What if I printed off a year-to-view calendar for Libby to use? All 365 days marked on one A4 page. That way I could circle some key dates like Christmas, her birthday, and Easter; as long as she knew where we were up to in the year, she had a clear visual so she could see how far away she was from key dates. So, I found a year-to-view calendar online, printed it off and circled the important days. As we weren't actually at the start of the year, I crossed off all the days that were already gone so Libby could see where we were up to, then I tried to explain to Libby how it worked the best that I could. I got a bit of Blu-tak and stuck the calendar up on the wall next to her desk where she sat each day.

The next morning, Libby came downstairs, took a red marker out of the drawer and crossed off the new day. The morning after that she did the same. And still, years later, the first thing Libby does, every single day, is take a red marker and cross today off on her calendar. When she was in hospital, we had to take the calendar there and stick it on the wall next to her bed so she could carry on crossing the days off.

What we did next was to give her a clearer day to day focus by making an A4 calendar for the current month to go alongside her year-to-view calendar. Using words and pictures, I would add significant events to the monthly calendar, like birthdays of family members, special days, visits to the doctor or dentist, trips out that were planned and, of course, visits to KFC. Without fail, every Saturday had a little clipart picture of a red and white striped bucket of chicken on it. When Libby moved to her new home at Oak, we marked her calendar to show when she could expect visits to Oak by Mum and Dad, or when she would be coming home for the weekend, so she also had a clear idea of how long she had to wait to see her family again. This calendar also got the days crossed off by Libby each morning.

Very quickly, these calendars became an essential part of Libby's life. She would start asking for her new monthly calendar well before the end of the current month. She knows the names of the months of the year by heart and knows which one comes next. Libby also knows that making the calendars on the computer falls under the heading of the slightly techy geeky stuff that Dad does. So, halfway through July, when she's home for the weekend, Libby will start to come up to me and say, 'August Calendar?' And mime making a cross in the air with a pen. I will then need to assure her that, yes, Dad will make a calendar for August before she goes back to Oak. These calendars now include little pictures of any presents that Libby has requested, so she knows exactly which day she can expect a new DVD, or whatever it might be.

In fact, Libby quite often likes to sit with me while the calendar is being made so she can be sure that Dad is getting everything down on the day that she expects it. Given that it's not easy to have conversations with Libby, I do rather enjoy these little negotiations.

Dad: Right, Hercules Soundtrack CD on Monday, yes?

Libby: (Pauses for a few seconds while she thinks) On Sunday.

Dad: Ah, you want it on Sunday?

Libby: On Sunday

Dad moves the photo of the Hercules CD to the Sunday

Dad: OK, Hercules CD on Sunday, yes?

Libby: Hercules CD on Sunday.

Dad: Yes?

Libby: Yes.

This system has really helped Libby understand when to expect things, but it has also done something we couldn't have originally envisioned at all. It has taught her patience. Within reason, put a date that something is going to happen on Libby's calendar and she is quite happy to wait until that day for it to happen. If, for example, Libby has been asking to go swimming, you don't have to tell her that she can go tomorrow to keep her happy. You can put that trip off for another few weeks, if you wanted to, by putting her swimming activity on her calendar in a few weeks time, perhaps with a little clipart picture of someone swimming. Libby can then see, every time she looks at her calendar (and she looks at it every day), that her swimming trip is going to happen, and she knows that every day she is getting closer to it. There's just one proviso to this strategy, though; if you've put something on the calendar, if you've said it's going to happen, then it better damn well happen.

Carers at Libby's residence who get to know her get to understand how her mind works and they get to understand this calendar system. It's really useful for them to help keep Libby from having any meltdowns. Her demands aren't usually unreasonable, so staff have learned that they can say yes, but they don't have to do what she has asked for on that day. They do need to tell her when it's going to happen, mind you, and, if possible, write it on her calendar. Libby knows that, once it's on her calendar, as far as she's concerned, it's written in stone and she can rely on that event happening. That is very comforting for her.

The downside of this is when staff are looking after Libby and they either don't know her very well, or they have failed to understand how this principle works. So, let's say Libby asks to go to the supermarket to buy some Pepsi, her favourite. Perhaps the transport at the house isn't available to take her that day, which is quite possible and fair enough, so the carer in question tells Libby that she can go to the supermarket tomorrow instead. Libby won't just casually accept this; she'll make sure that this has been negotiated in full. 'First sleep', she'll tell her staff, 'then, supermarket shopping for Pepsi.' She'll wait for her carer to confirm this and then she'll say it again: 'First sleep, then super-market shopping for Pepsi', then she'll toddle off, quite satisfied with this arrangement, maybe repeating this a few times as she walks away, just to reassure herself.

And then, tomorrow comes, and the inexperienced or unthinking staff member doesn't sort out the transport, and when Libby asks about going to the supermarket, she gets a rather glib reply of, 'Oh, we can't go today, Libby, we'll have to go another time.' Just one problem there, buster. Libby is autis-tic, and you know she is because you're her carer and it's your job to cater for her because of her needs. And if you mess with her mind like that, she's going to have a meltdown. So when she's kicking off big time because you said something was going to happen today and now it isn't, don't be surprised. Don't go around showing everyone the bruise you got off Libby like you've been hard done by; you made this happen. You can't fob Libby off with saying something might happen 'another time'. If what she's asking for can be done, then tell her when and put it on her calendar for her. It's OK if it can't happen for a while, she'll generally be pretty understanding of that. Then make sure it happens. If what's she's asking for isn't doable, don't just blag her with vague promises. Tell her, as nicely as you can, that we can't do that right now. Again, she'll be more understanding than you think.

Libby processes what is happening in her day to day life by what is on her calendar. It was a fantastic breakthrough that, to this day, I am rather proud of myself for initiating. It was a moment of top dadding. But if you live by the calendar, you die by the calendar. Use it wisely, to give Libby's life order, and you won't have to be ruled by her demands. She'll go along with more or less whatever you say and is happy to run to your timetable, as long as it's on her calendar. But don't even think about ignoring something on the calendar and just hope that she'll forget. Once something is on that calendar, Libby becomes like an elephant. She will trample all over you in a highly violent manner if you don't do what it says. Oh, and she won't forget, either.

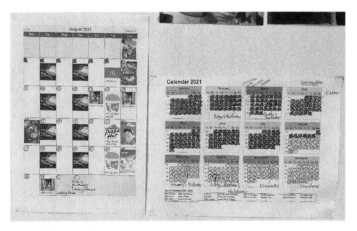

Libby's monthly and year to view calendars that she marks with a red cross everyday

The fact that Libby is Mum's girl meant, of course, that Robyn ended up being Daddy's Little Girl. Even at 23. At first, she will have just gone along with what was happening. Libby is always with Mum, so I'll stay with Dad. But, over time, this has definitely become her preference. To give you an example: my new job means that I finish my shifts very late, often getting in not long before midnight. When Robyn comes home for the weekend, I will always make sure I am there for the main days of her stay, but I might be in work when she arrives in the evening on the first night. However, she won't go to bed until I get in from work. Karen will tell me that she will have been slightly unsettled all evening, and she has constantly been reassuring her that Daddy will be home soon. And then, when I arrive home, she is suddenly all smiles and ready to settle for the night.

Robyn may not talk, but her smiles and snuggles can be so comforting during tough times. I'm a football fan and I support Tottenham Hotspur. Feel free to make your jokes; I've heard them all and made most of them myself. Over the years I've had to learn not to get too down about Spurs defeats. There's really no point in being miserable about the result of a sports event, either with yourself or those around you. When Tottenham reached the European Champions' League Final in 2019, I invited friends round for a party. I was determined to enjoy the experience because being a Spurs fan means these events don't come along very often and you must always assume that defeat is inevitable. I wasn't wrong, but I wasn't devastated at the final whistle, either. I had prepared myself for defeat.

I wasn't always this good at footballing self-care, and I used to get really fed up about Tottenham losing. Fans of the English Premier League may recall the end of the 2006 season and what became known as Lasagne-gate. Spurs only needed to win their final game of the season to qualify for the European Champions' League for the first time in their history. On the day of the game, many Spurs players seemingly came down with food poisoning due to a famous dodgy lasagne they had all eaten the night before (it was actually just a virus that spread through the team, but that's not nearly as entertaining and so gets forgotten about). The club tried to get the game postponed, but the Premier

League weren't about to allow that to happen. The players went out to play after throwing up before hand and even during the game itself. Unsurprisingly, they were defeated 2-1 by West Ham. At the same time, their dreaded rivals Arsenal won their final game of the season to take Tottenham's place in the Champions' League. It was a perfectly galling footballing storm.

I was absolutely gutted. In fact, it may well have been this experience that taught me that getting upset about the results of football matches just wasn't worth it, and this was where I began to develop my ability to just quickly put defeats to one side. I went upstairs to our bedroom and just lay on our bed with my face buried in my pillow, cursing my luck, and also cursing myself for choosing stupid Spurs as my team as a child. And as I lay there, I heard the door open and quiet footsteps walking across the room. Then I felt someone climbing on the bed. It was 8 year-old Robyn. She put her head on the pillow next to mine and put her arms around me. That's fairly everyday for Robyn now, but it was actually slightly unusual for her to do that at the time. I turned my head to the side that she was on to look at her, and she just gave me a big Robyn smile.

It was a lovely moment. A classic 'puts everything into perspective' event. I don't know how much she knew about how I felt. Did she want to cheer me up as she knew how down I was? Or was she just wanting some attention from her Dad? At a time like that, it's important not to worry about why, and just take the happy moment that the universe has given you. Who cares about football when I have this wonderful girl? Why be bothered about the Champions' League when I have this smiling face and beautiful eyes in front of me, and this daughter of mine wants nothing more than a snuggle with her Dad? I'll never forget how unimportant a football result felt in that minute. When it came to a comparison of importance of watching sport and my lovely Robyn, it wasn't even close. I'll never forget what she taught me that day, just by wanting to be next to me.

❧ 4 ❧

HUNGRY LIKE THE WOLF - FOOD
PRESENT DAY

T his was the first blog post I wrote. Well, technically, the Disneyland posts were written first, but they were just written as a bit of an exercise to see if I could write about the girls in an interesting way. This was the first thing I had written deliberately to post as a blog. It was short, only 350 words, and it lacked the purpose of later posts when I had warmed to my theme of a paternal storyteller of autistic tales. Here I'm just commenting on one of the oddities of life with autistic kids. It's interesting that the first thing I chose to write about was food, though, because it's always been a crucial issue with the girls.

BLOG POST FROM JANUARY 15 2011 - HUNGRY HEART

Robyn loves chilli, bolognese and curry with rice. Lots of rice. She's a picky eater, but what she eats, she eats in large amounts. Seriously large amounts.

What I want to know is this. Is it normal for a very average sized 12 year-old to eat this much food? I like my food, and if I'm in the mood I can put away a couple of those adult sized pasta bowls of one of Robyn's favourites. But Robyn will eat 3 or 4 bowls, every scrap, and still ask for more. I don't think I could eat that much if you put a gun to my head.

Let me reiterate, Robyn is a very normal healthy size – not overweight at all. But just today she had an adult dinner sized serving of Bolognese with rice. For breakfast. Then she headed out for the morning with a care worker, and while she was gone I converted the Bolognese into a chilli by adding kidney beans and chilli powder. She came in and has eaten two large bowls of this with rice. She is standing next to me right now, holding out a bowl that is devoid of a single grain of rice. Only the slightest brown/orange smear on the bowl would give you any indication that, 5 minutes ago, this bowl contained enough food to keep most adults happy.

Of course, I'm telling her that she really doesn't need anymore; that she's had plenty. Robyn won't back down, though. She'll just stand there repeatedly shoving that smelly bowl into my face until I give up and get her another huge bowl of chilli. And Robyn knows I will tire of her bothering me long before she gets tired of bothering me.

A responsible parent would stand firm. A responsible parent would withstand all this badgering knowing that, in the long term, giving in would mean impending obesity for their beloved offspring. However, this is me. If the Good Lord didn't want Robyn to eat 5 massive bowls of chilli in one day, he should have sent her to someone else.

PRESENT DAY

The general tone was there, wasn't it? I'm lacking seriousness in my way of discussing autism, which is my M.O., and I'm quite unapologetic of my parenting style. You could see where I was headed. Friends reassured me that I could afford to be a bit more verbose. The word count crept up until the blogs were more like 1,000-1,500 words, but I was very wary of boring people at the start.

It's worth pointing out that Robyn is still very slim, though she doesn't eat quite as much as she used to; her metabolism seems to have calmed down somewhat.

MacBook and curry while wrapped in her blanket is a
perfect combination for Robyn

BLOG POST FROM FEBRUARY 18 2011 - EAT TO THE BEAT

The older I get, the more I love my food. My ever increasing waistline is a testament to this, as is my reluctance to go on any form of date with my wife that isn't a visit to a restaurant. I am of the opinion that the cinema, for instance, is an inappropriate place to go to spend time with your significant other. We don't get to spend nearly as much time together as we would like, and a trip to the movies does not allow you to talk or interact in any significant way. Also, crucially, none of the food they serve has been deep-fried.

I think I've probably passed this passion onto my children. I've already written here about the sheer, mind blowing amounts of food that Robyn can tuck away, but it's the types of food the girls choose to eat, rather than the amount, that I wish to address here. My Mum has never had much respect for the opinions of doctors in regard to childcare. Accepted wisdom in the medical community when we had our babies is that they should not have anything but milk to eat for their first two months of life. Given the fact that our eminent physicians change their mind about what is and isn't appropriate for babies approximately every eight minutes, it's unsurprising that Mum gives their opinions short shrift. This attitude should be borne in mind when I tell you that she would cuddle a two week old Robyn and soothe her by letting her suck on her finger. That had been dipped in curry.

Robyn then, seems to have gained a taste for the spicy stuff long before her first tooth had appeared, and Liberty was no different. Curry is still their favourite food, though they have different ways of approaching it. Libby doesn't eat mushrooms, but they are Robyn's very favourite thing in the world. Consider that for a moment; a kid who is an unbelievably fussy eater whose favourite food is one of the classic foods that kids refuse to eat: mushrooms. That's my daughter. However, this is a complete winner for our son George as he, rather more typically, can't stand mushrooms. So when he dumps all his mushrooms onto Robyn's plate, he isn't actually being fussy and turning his nose up at healthy vegetables. No, he is actually a caring brother who is making sure that his special needs little sister gets as much of her favourite food as possible. What a lovely boy he is!

Then there's the rice. Rice is Robyn's carbohydrate of choice. Liberty also favours rice, but will happily tuck into pasta and potatoes as long as she likes what's being served with them, but it's rice only for Robyn. So when we all have bolognese and pasta, Robyn will have bolognese and rice. A few years ago my Mum was making a cottage pie with minced beef and mashed potato (another big Libby favourite by the way). Some way into making the dish, having watched Mum cook the minced beef, onions and carrots, Robyn decided she didn't like the way mum's recipe was progressing. She rooted around in the kitchen cupboards for a while and brought several cans of chopped tomatoes to mum. So, instead of serving her family a Cottage Pie as she had planned, mum had to serve up bolognese. With rice. And carrots.

Something else about the rice. We eat Sunday dinner with extended family members (which is why my Mum is featuring heavily in this edition!), sometimes having a Sunday roast, but sometimes other things, too. When Mum made curry she always cooked basmati rice to accompany it. Robyn soon decided that she liked this more expensive rice option so much that we had to start eating it at home, too. So now, every rice based meal Chez Dickenson (and there are plenty of them) come with the tastier, swankier basmati option as standard. Good work, Robyn!

It's funny how small acts can have larger consequences. On that Sunday afternoon when we allowed Mum to start feeding curry to a two week old Robyn, I'm sure we didn't imagine that it *would mean that we would have to eat curry and rice at least once a week for the next decade or more. But we have. And with some naan bread, poppadoms and mango chutney, we still like it, too.*

Next week we will celebrate Robyn's 13th birthday with all of the family coming over for dinner. No prizes for guessing what's on the menu.

This was the day I got my new iPad. It was covered in curry within minutes of its arrival

FOOD UPDATE: ROBYN STILL LOVES CURRY AND, WHEN WE HAVE A party for her birthday, it's always a curry party. True, we do swank it up a bit for her guests by making sure we have lots of Indian trimmings such as Bombay Potatoes, Samosas, Naan, Poppadoms, etc. Not that Robyn eats anything more than her Korma and Basmati Rice, but it means the party theme is something she can join in, whereas if we had classic party nibbles she wouldn't touch them. Oddly, though, mushrooms have gone from her absolute favourite thing to ingredient non grata. Don't try making Robyn a curry with mushrooms anymore; she doesn't want to know. I actually tried her with it recently, chopping the mushrooms reasonably fine so as to ease her back into it and remind her that they were her favourite, but all I did was ruin a batch of curry because she refused to eat it.

BLOG POST FROM APRIL 2₃ 2011 - CHOCOLATE GIRL

It's Easter weekend, so I feel I should write something appropriate to the upcoming festivities. Given that the girls' understanding of religious matters is less than sketchy, that leaves us with only one place to go: chocolate.

Liberty loves her chocolate and has a fantastic capacity to consume it. You know how you think you can eat chocolate all day and then, after a while, you feel a bit sick and realise you can't? It's like you have a natural inbuilt limiter that tells you that you don't need anymore sweet things. Well, like lots of other things, Libby doesn't have one of those. If there's a big slab of Cadbury's Dairy Milk in the fridge, then Libby will just work her way through the entire thing unless somebody hides it. If it makes her feel at all sick then she isn't letting on.

Liberty loves special holiday celebrations, and Easter is no exception. We have an Easter egg hunt in our garden with our kids and all of our nieces and nephews and some family friends. Libby enjoys the combination of bustle from all the guests and other kids in the house, and getting many, many 'chocolate eggs' (I write the words in quotation marks because that's what Libby calls them rather than Creme Eggs or whatever; she loves her chocolate eggs). Libby joins in with gusto, living out her wildest dreams, rushing around the garden gathering far too many eggs, not quite able to believe her luck that, for one day in the year, chocolate eggs are available just lying around the garden for free. Other parents keep an eye on their kids to make sure they don't take too many eggs and leave plenty for the other kids. 'The other kids' seeming mostly to be Liberty who gets twice as many eggs as everyone else.

Libby finds an Easter egg on top of the shed

During all this excitement, Robyn, typically, sits on a chair watching a movie on her iPad, headphones on, ignoring every-thing around her. You see, Robyn doesn't really like fuss. Or chocolate. Or rather, she does, but only in very specific circum-stances, and this is one of my very favourite Robyn quirks. Give Robyn an Easter egg, a bar of chocolate, Chocolate Orange, Mars Bar, Kitkat or Snickers and she will show zero level of inter-est. However, if you give Robyn a Magnum ice cream (which is a block of vanilla ice cream encased in Belgian chocolate on a stick), despite shunning all other chocolate previously, she will sit down and carefully crack the chocolate and peel it away from the ice cream, eating every last scrap as if chocolate was the greatest invention since the wheel.

Now, some of you are probably thinking that it must be the

Belgian chocolate that Walls use on their Magnums that she is especially partial to. But, no. Cadbury's make a product that is identical, other than obviously using Cadbury's chocolate instead, and if you give Robyn one of those she is just as happy. Hell, give her an Iceland 'Majestic', the generic rip-off of a Magnum, and she'll lovingly peel away all the chocolate and scoff it down. Oh, and regardless of what brand it is, as soon as she's finished the chocolate, she'll give you back the ice cream as she's not interested in that at all. So when we go into a shop for a treat and Robyn selects a Magnum, you buy it for her knowing it will make her happy, but also you're aware that, Belgian or not, at £1.50 for about an ounce, this is some of the worst value chocolate in the world.

It's the Big Easter Egg Hunt, but Robyn is just wandering around the garden with a laptop and headphones

Most of the supermarkets in the UK sell a double chocolate chip cookie that you buy in little bags of five. They are big, soft, chocolate cookies with lots of chocolate chips in; lovely stuff. Both Robyn and Libby like these and we sometimes buy the girls a bag of them to share over the weekend. My recollection is that Robyn used to eat these in their entirety, but now she's decided she only really likes the chocolate chips. This means that in sorting out the cookie from the chips Robyn makes an unholy mess. Cleaning up all these cookie remnants is a pain, though given how much she leaves behind it does pay dividends as, if the mood takes you, you get to eat big clumps of chocolate cookie as you go. A word of caution, though: when Robyn is in one of her stages where she is smearing poo around the house, you have to approach clearing up and eating her chocolate cookie leftovers with extreme caution. Enough said.

So, what to drink with their favourite treats? Both drink Schweppes Lemonade, but won't drink other brands. No cheapo supermarket brands for my daughters, which is a shame as the generic brands are a fraction of the price of Schweppes. Many of you will know that I don't drink alcohol, but I do like to indulge in the occasional glass of caffeinated cola; my nights don't get any crazier than that. Pepsi is my cola brand of choice; it's sweeter and less fizzy than Coke, which is to my taste. Irresponsible and downright stupid as it may be, we have allowed our kids to occasionally indulge in the good stuff as well. Libby will drink either major brand, though she calls it all 'Pepsi' even if it comes with a red label, because that's what we usually have at home. Robyn, unsurprisingly, is much more choosy.

Robyn, Dad and Mum clink Pepsi bottles whilst out for a meal

My friend Spike shares my love of a cola beverage and, like me, will drink either of the major brands, but his preference is for Coke. On one memorable occasion a few years ago, we were visiting his house where we were eating Chinese food with Spike, his wife Kate and their kids. Spike had poured himself a glass of Coke and put it on the side in the kitchen. Robyn entered the room, spied a glass of the black gold and picked it up, ready to drink. Spike and I shared a look as she went to drink from the glass. Robyn is so picky about her food and drink, but we had always figured that a lot of it was about the pictures and colours on the label. Robyn, unknowingly, was about to take the Pepsi Challenge. Would she be able to tell the difference?

She grasped the glass in her hands and took a big gulp of what she thought was her favourite drink. Spike and I smiled at each other, knowing that she'd been fooled. She couldn't really tell the difference at all. Take away the red label and she would be just as happy to drink cola made by Coke as their dreaded rivals. But, after a moment, Robyn fixed us with a look that can only be described as contemptuous. Then she opened her mouth and let the Coke dribble slowly from her mouth onto the floor. She left the room and left us to clear up after her. Well, it served us right, thinking we could fool a young autistic kid into thinking Coca-cola was Pepsi. When will we ever truly realise how smart Robyn is?

PRESENT DAY

It's a very recent development, but Robyn will now actually eat all of a Magnum. She enjoys ice cream in general much more than she used to but, in a classic Robyn move, she usually only eats expensive Ben & Jerry's ice cream. If ever we take a tub out of the freezer while watching a movie or something, Robyn will suddenly become very interested and sit next to us, so we have to share our ice cream with her.

Another ice cream foible she has is how she eats a Twister. A Twister, for those whose lives have not been blessed with their deliciousness, is a twisty lemon fruit ice and pineapple ice cream with a strawberry ice core. I know what you're thinking; the strawberry and lemon twisty ice bits sound fine, but does that pineapple ice cream twisted around it really work? Well, if your name is Robyn, then no, it absolutely doesn't. She loves a Twister, but not until Mum or Dad has sat down with a spoon and carefully scraped all traces of pineapple ice cream off so she can just eat the fruity ice bit. It's fiddly and messy, but these are the lengths that we are willing to go to keep our little girl happy.

Robyn and Libby enjoying a KFC picnic on a Saturday lunchtime

Another piece of unhealthy food eating is the girls' trips to KFC. I'm not sure when it started, but every Saturday is KFC day. And I mean every damn Saturday. Like a lot of people, I don't mind a piece or two of KFC's original recipe chicken with its special blend of eleven herbs and spices. Well, I didn't used to mind it, but now I'm heartily sick of it. If you went to the same food emporium every single Saturday, week after week, year after year, you'll find you'd get pretty sick of it, too. Robyn and Libby never do, though, and Libby counts down every week until her Saturday treat: 'KFC! 3 pieces of chicken, 2 more sleeps! Big Pepsi, 2 more sleeps!' I've tried a few things off the menu over the years to keep me interested. I went through a phase of eating the fries with a carton of beans. Chips and beans is not remotely a KFC dish, so that worked for a while, but I got fed up of that in the end as well. I can now sit at a table in KFC and watch Libby and Robyn eat piece after piece of fried chicken and not feel the slightest inclination to join in.

Food was a major problem when Robyn finally left high school at 19, and she got a place at a college for students with additional needs. She was there for two years; one year staying at one of the residences on campus, and the other year at a shared house in a small nearby town. The college was about 40 minutes away from where we live, and Robyn would come home every weekend. Before Robyn began her course, we had to fill in endless forms to explain about Robyn's behaviours, interests and preferences. This included explaining in detail about Robyn's limited diet. Robyn still mainly eats rice with three options: curry, bolognese and chilli. Then there are a number of other bits and pieces she'll eat, like bacon or chicken dippers. So, it was important to get that kind of information over to new carers or she'd end up not eating at all!

It took hours to get all that information down but, of course, we provided them with all the detail they would need. But information coming back from college in the early weeks of her course said that she was off her food and was losing weight. And then we found out why. We realised that those whose job it was to take care of her at college seemed to think the information we'd provided about her diet wasn't a strict set of rules but 'more what you'd call guidelines'. Random meals were being made for her. Similar to when she was at high school, a record was written for how she got on every day, and one day we read, 'Robyn didn't touch her cheese sandwich.' Her what? Cheese sandwich? Does Robyn eat cheese? Ever? Well, technically, yes. She eats a cheeseburger from McDonald's. But a cheese sandwich? In what world did someone think that Robyn was going to eat a cheese sandwich? Clearly, one where people weren't paying any attention to the handover information they'd been given.

In fact, when we enquired about the booklets we'd painstakingly filled in, no one seemed to know where they were. The cheese sandwich was the famous example, but they basically weren't catering to her requirements at all. For instance, Robyn drinks lemonade, but we know she only drinks Schweppes lemonade, not diet own brand lemonade from Aldi, and you don't need to be some sort of lemonade sommelier to tell the difference between those two. This had all been explained in detail.

Robyn continued to be unhappy and lose weight, and she wasn't exactly a bloater to begin with. Every time she came home she looked increasingly emaciated and we were on the verge of pulling her out of college. It was then that a guardian angel by the name of Hannah appeared. Hannah was paired with Robyn as a carer at her residence and just seemed to immediately 'get' Robyn. Hannah understood Robyn's needs and how there was little room for manoeuvre with them. It was surprising that more staff didn't understand that, considering that there were a good number of autistic students in the college. Hannah made sure that Robyn was getting the right food, and even when she wasn't on shift, that better understanding of Robyn's requirements rubbed off on the other staff in their house. Hannah understood more than just Robyn's basic needs, though. She understood her personality and character; she was able to be her friend and help her to settle and enjoy college. Hannah was an absolute godsend and we will always be hugely grateful for how she helped Robyn.

Robyn and her Carer/Guardian Angel, Hannah

5

THIS IS WHY WE CAN'T HAVE NICE THINGS - TECHNOLOGY

BLOG POST FROM APRIL 1 2011 - COMPUTER
LOVE

If you don't actually know my daughters then you won't find their love of technology and their ability to use it to be surprising. Therefore, you need to bear in mind the following; these girls do not really speak. They can't properly dress themselves. If you weren't there to remind them, they would happily throw their fork aside and eat curry with their bare hands. They are nocturnally incontinent. They would think nothing of disrobing and running around naked in public if you weren't there to discourage them, and both girls are now reaching puberty. However, put the latest iGadget in front of them and they don't need to even glance at an instruction manual, not that it would do them much good if they did.

The iPod was where it first began. I bought my first one in around 2005; an original Classic with a click wheel. For fun, I decided to upload some Disney songs to it and put some old-fashioned head-hugging headphones on Robyn to see if she responded. She loved it, and so did we. Not only did we have a new activity that Robyn enjoyed, it was completely portable and something she could use whilst we were out and about to help keep her calm. Looking back, this was a major breakthrough for *us. Soon she didn't need much help to operate it either, as she quickly got to grips with the click-wheel controls.*

Her love of technology didn't always mean a positive experience for everyone else, mind you. Robyn was never satisfied with just putting her iPod down when she had finished listening. She always had to unplug the headphones and then throw the iPod across the room to signify that she was done with Disney tunes for now, thank you very much. In a carpeted house this wasn't usually too disastrous for the iPod, but I remember her doing it in church on a number of occasions. Apparently, launching your iPod across a chapel so it hits people several pews further along is not generally considered to be appropriate behaviour in the Lord's house.

Then there's Libby's insistence on microwaving her own popcorn. She knows how to put the popcorn bag in, she knows to press 'TIME' and then some numbers and then press 'START'; she's just a bit sketchy on what exactly those numbers should be. So when she sets microwave popcorn to cook for 88 minutes when her mum and dad are in bed, there are two outcomes: 1) a house that smells so badly of burnt popcorn that it needs aerating for days, and 2) we have to buy a new microwave oven.

When it comes to computers, I think they learned their initial abilities at school. They were obviously taught how to use a mouse there and were then able to bring these skills home with them. I remember my surprise and delight at seeing Robyn operating our computer with confidence for the first time. Given her complete lack of understanding of the world she lives in, I didn't dream that she would be able to get her head around such a concept. But she did, and Liberty quickly followed.

Those who are familiar with computers will know that Macs and PCs have different operating systems. We use Macs at home, and when people ask me if it's difficult to change over to a Mac, I always tell them it's like getting a new car; it does all the same things your old car did, just differently and, although some of the buttons and methods of operation will be new to you, you'll quickly get used to it. (There usually follows some dig about your old car being a Nissan Micra and your new one being a Ferrari, but I won't bother with that here.) However, I know quite a few adults who have found the changeover frustrating. Given this state of affairs, one might think that Robyn and Liberty would find the difference between the Windows based PCs at school and the Macs we use at home to be utterly baffling. But it's never fazed them in the slightest. They can use iTunes, Photo Booth, the internet and play simple games without any problems at all.

Robyn still likes to sit up high. Here she relaxes on
the shed roof with her laptop

I can remember very clearly the day I got my iPad. Like the Apple geek that I am, I had said gadget on pre-order, and it actually arrived the day before they were supposed to be released. However, we then went away for the weekend so I *didn't get to show it to Robyn for a few days, but I was really looking forward to sitting down with my eldest daughter to show her how to use this new cutting edge piece of kit. When we got home I called Robyn over and sat her on my knee with the iPad. I switched it on, and with a swipe of my finger, it sprang to life. I was really excited to show her how she could listen to music, play fun games and watch movies and YouTube without using a mouse or a keyboard. She allowed me to show her how every-thing worked for all of five seconds before she took it out of my hands and began using it with a dexterity that I still don't have a year later. I was deprived of a bonding moment, but given a new sense of admiration for her abilities. Liberty is just as adept at using new technology, with the added bonus of being able to spell complex words to aid her in her internet searches, but more of that another time.*

Libby watching The Snowman on the iMac

Some of you will be thinking that we must be made of money (let me assure you we are not). Not necessarily because we can afford all this technology, but because we let our rather careless daughters run around using it. Well, along with accepting their condition, you really have to accept the consequences of what comes with it. If I was to get stressed every time Libby and Robyn broke something of value, I would have been dead of a heart attack a long time ago. They have broken expensive items on many occasions, and we have learned over time not to get upset or angry about it; there's no point in being precious about objects that can be replaced. Such events are generally accompanied by a heavy sigh and a phone call to the insurance company. Needless to say we have the most comprehensive housing and contents cover known to man.

PRESENT DAY

Just something to add in regard to matters technological. I'm a keen Facebooker, and Facebook was a good place to keep family up to date with the goings on of Robyn and Libby. George and Karen obviously had their own accounts, but I was the one who tended to post photos and stories about the girls. It did leave me to wonder, sometimes, if I wasn't making too many posts to my timeline, and were all of my Facebook friends that interested in what was going on in the lives of my teenage autistic daughters? So, I came up with the idea of creating an account for each of the girls for sharing photos, stories and information pertaining to them. What it also meant was that only people who knew Robyn and Libby had to make a friend request; others who weren't interested didn't have to bother reading about them anymore.

Libby now has 92 Facebook friends and Robyn has 101, so it seems there are plenty of family and friends who are interested in what they've got going on. I write the posts in the first person and try to convey something of what I feel is their personality in their posts. Robyn is always portrayed as funny and cheeky and finds her little sister a bit of a pain. Libby likes to talk about the presents she has received and how frequently she gets to go to her favourite fast food emporia. I've obviously been fairly successful in creating their Facebook personae, as friends who know Karen and me better than they actually know Robyn and Libby have sometimes commented on how surprised they are that the girls can write so well. I have to let them know that even though Libby can type words into a computer, it is only usually the names of films, characters and YouTube videos, rather than her thoughts and feelings about her day to day life, and Robyn isn't able to write at all.

BLOG POST FROM JULY 2011 - PAPA'S GOT A BRAND NEW BAG

There's an episode of The Simpsons where Homer tries to buy a camper van for his family. The sales guy agrees to sell him a top of the line model on a 'buy now, pay later' scheme, but when he puts Homer's name into the computer, buzzers and sirens go off to indicate that Mr Simpson is not entirely suited to such a premium line of credit. This has not happened to me when buying something on credit, but I am constantly surprised that something similar does not happen when I buy insurance. For many people, insurance of all kinds is not a particularly good investment. You pay moderate sums of money over a long period of time that can eventually add up to huge sums of money, for which most people get very little return. Personally though, if I had to choose one word to describe the concept of insurance, it would be this one: awesome.

Robyn is happily playing on my new iPad 2 that arrived yesterday. After a lot of typical Dickenson House wear and tear, my original iPad died the other week. Of course, we are covered with Robyn & Libby Special Insurance, so a quick call to my insurer and they picked it up to fix it. As it was beyond economical repair, they sent me a healthy sized cheque for the full amount of a new iPad 2, minus the £50 excess charge. Bob's your uncle, Fanny's your aunt, I'm now up to the minute with the latest Apple gear. But surely, I hear you say, given the sheer volume of breakages in your house, you can't claim on your house contents insurance for everything your daughters break, can you? Well, no. We don't do that. What we do is this: you know when you buy something in shops, particularly electrical items, and they say something like, 'Would you like to extend the guarantee on that to three years for an extra £24.99' or whatever? You say, 'No thanks', right? I do consider my answer carefully first, but quite often my answer is, 'Yes. Yes, please.'

You see, these extended guarantees cover you for any fault to your product that occurs over the three years but, crucially, they also cover you for accidental damage. Of course, what constitutes an accident can vary from house to house. In most houses that means that only if something is broken unintentionally are you covered. Well, I don't live in most houses; I live in a house with Robyn and Libby. That's right, the rules are different for us; even if my girls get bored with a product and throw it at the wall, because of their condition that's technically an accident and the policy says I can have a brand new one.

I bought my first iPod in 2006 and bought the insurance cover for it at my favourite store, Argos. Michael McIntyre may mock the place, but I love Argos. Argos is where they sell you extended warranties on electrical items that are considerably cheaper than those you buy in proper electrical stores. And, because their sales assistants have practically zero knowledge of electrical goods, when I take my iPod back and say, 'This is broken, I need a new one', they just go and get me one without even trying to switch the broken iPod on. It wouldn't matter if they did check; the thing really is broken, but it's quite pleasant not to have to deal with the third degree every time the girls break something. Most of the time, they don't even sell you a new policy.

So, allow me to make this quite clear for you. You buy a product, let's say an iPod. It breaks not long after because Libby leaves it on the trampoline outside all night and it rains (true story, more than once). You can't return it under the original guarantee from Apple because it's your fault. But you can return it to Argos if you paid extra to extend your guarantee and to cover accidental damage. So they give you a new one. And that guarantee you bought originally is still valid. So, you happily take home your brand new iPod. One day, a couple of months later, Robyn has a tantrum, throws your iPod and smashes it on the corner of a wooden chair. So you take it back to Argos, they give you a new one, and my original guarantee is still valid. With just one policy that I bought for about 30 quid, I was able to take my iPod back six times to get a brand new one. That's six new iPods for the princely sum of thirty of your English Pounds, people.

I am not being in any way dishonest; I am covered for accidental damages and I just happen to have two little cherubs who have lots of accidents. This is just a system that works poorly for most, but very well for us. I must confess, however, that I have taken to making use of the number of different Argos stores in our area when I take things back. They may have thousands of customers, but I think they're starting to recognise me now, and it's getting a bit embarrassing. 'Hi, yeah, it's me with the autistic kids, again. Sorry, I'll be needing another iPod/DVD player/pair of headphones/toaster/microwave oven/computer keyboard/kettle/hairdryer/fridge freezer/steam generator iron/laptop computer.' Yes, we have had every single one of those items replaced on an extended guarantee, some of them more than once.

(Present Day: This was an accurate portrayal of the situation at that time. However, Argos did not remain this inept forever and, eventually, they enacted some returns policies that were more in line with those that you might get in other electrical stores. However, their rather lax procedures saw us through some of the girls' most destructive years, so cheers for that, Argos, and I'm sorry if Robyn and Libby negatively affected your share price over that time.)

We're not the only people who need to be insured because of the girls, either. Recently, Karen and I were having something of a well-earned lie-in, thinking that the children were all sleeping soundly in their beds. It turned out that Robyn wasn't sleeping at all and had, in fact, escaped. A knock on the door awoke us from our sleep. Karen went down to answer the door and it was our friend the farmer; Robyn had fancied playing in cow poo again, this time at the crack of dawn. Normally we are quickly alerted to her escapes but, due to us being asleep, this one caught us on the hop. The farmer was very pleasant and understanding about the situation, which is always a relief for us in these circumstances.

However, a week or so later the farmer came back to the house, still being very genial, to tell us the full details of Robyn's most recent escape. In her adventures with the cows, she had left a gate open that had allowed some of the cows to escape their pen. They had gone into areas where they weren't to go, with floors that were not suitable for cows to walk on. A calf had done the splits on all four of its legs on the slippy floor, couldn't get up and had to be put down. On its own, this is a sad tale of a poor cow that died, and I did feel genuinely sad for the poor blighter. But the farmer wasn't here just to make us feel bad. He had to get details about Robyn's condition so he could make a full report to his insurer. It turns out the young bull was worth up to £10,000!

In the circumstances, the farmer would have been justified in being upset with us for allowing Robyn to escape to the farm unsupervised with terminal consequences for his cow. However, he was very understanding, just needing information from us for his insurance claim. Some people have got all kinds of mad at us for our daughters' actions, without being remotely as inconvenienced as our good farmer friend. He taught us all something of a lesson about not judging and having compassion and understanding, even with Robyn the cow killer. It was one of those situations that isn't really anyone's fault, but that didn't stop Karen and I from feeling terribly guilty about the poor calf and that the farmer that had to claim on his business insurance. Still, at least he was 10 grand up on the deal, eh?

Insurance does have its benefits, then. If you're a bit of a techy geek like me, it's always disappointing when companies come out with a new version of a product you already have. You've got your iPhone 3G and you're more than happy with it, and then they bring out a shiny new iPhone 4 and you're left feeling behind the times. I don't suffer from that feeling very often. When they announced the iPad 2, friends asked me, knowing of my predilection for all things Apple, if I was going to buy one when it came out. The answer was 'no'. I knew I didn't need to go out and buy one. I didn't need another iPad as the one I had was perfectly fine until it broke beyond repair. And in our house, 'broke beyond repair' is a situation that is never very far away.

Let me be clear, I have never deliberately broken an item because I fancied having a new one (let's be honest, I've never really needed to). It's just that we have a lot more 'accidents' than other people do. We also have a variety of insurance policies to spread our liabilities so one company doesn't take the hit all the time. We have extremely comprehensive home insurance, another policy called Safe2Go that insures all our portable items (they bought me my Macbook Pro after Robyn smashed my old Macbook – nice work, guys) and then we have individual extended guarantees on many less expensive items. I checked when I bought the new iPad this week how much a 3-year *warranty would be for it: £189. No, thanks. I'll just have to claim on one of my other policies if (when) it breaks again.*

You might think all this insurance costs a lot, and I'm sure it does add up. But it only costs a fraction of what we would pay to replace all these items that Robyn and Libby break with such nauseating regularity. There are many small sacrifices I have to make with my daughters, but insurance policies mean that I don't have to sacrifice all of my gadgets, and it also stops me from getting too cross with them or resentful about our situation when they break my stuff. In fact, thanks to the girls, I've always got the flashiest technology around. At least until those insurance guys get wise to me and the alarms start to go off in the shop when I agree to buy an extended guarantee...

Robyn wraps herself in her quilt whilst on the iMac

PRESENT DAY

Another way of providing Libby with continued access to portable entertainment was for her just to have someone else's. Obviously, I liked my iPad, but I also like living without pain, and I'm not going to have a pain free existence when Libby has deliberately smashed her iPad and is now upset because she has no iPad. You can try the no sympathy route, but then she starts beating you, and that's no fun. I found a Facebook status from 2014 that said:

'We had 4 iPads. I had one, so did Robyn, Libby and Karen had an iPad Mini. Libby smashed hers, so I gave her mine. Then she smashed the one I gave her, so we gave her Robyn's (and bought Robyn a nice new iPod instead). Today she has smashed the 3rd one, and now will inherit Karen's iPad Mini. Until she inevitably smashes that.'

Flat Screen TVs increased in popularity and decreased in price at a good time for us, and also for our insurance company. We got our first flat screen in 2006, but prior to that we had the old style boxes that everyone had back then. In the first three years in the house that we moved into in 2002, we had to claim on our insurance three times for a new television. Those old TVs are normally fairly reliable on their own, but less reliable when subjected to the behaviour of Robyn and Liberty. One of our televisions just seemed to stop working one day when the picture failed. When we took the back of the set off, we found that one of the girls had managed to slide a Refresher Chew Bar down one of the ventilation slots on the back. With the heat of the CRT tube, the Refresher Chew Bar had then melted all over it. Apparently, they don't work too well when that happens, so that meant a call to the insurance people and a new TV.

On another occasion, I had noticed that there was a crack in the plastic on the top of the TV, though I was clueless as to how it had got there. Then one day I found out. Libby was watching a

Disney film and really enjoying dancing to the soundtrack. Although, apparently, the optimum way to enjoy a Disney soundtrack is by actually dancing on top of the television set itself. I couldn't believe my eyes when I walked into the lounge to see her set top grooving and, obviously, quickly took her down. However, she clearly continued doing this whenever I wasn't around. I know this because, on another occasion, I walked in to find her trying to watch the television from her vantage point which was actually standing inside the set itself. Clearly, this time, her moves had been sufficiently enthusiastic to actually send her through the top of the TV. She hadn't cried or got upset about it, mind you, just leaned her head forward so she could carry on watching, albeit from a very odd angle.

Unsurprisingly, when we did buy our first plasma flat screen, we opted to have it fixed to the wall, in order to avoid anymore Libby based breakages, and that seemed to do the trick. We used that as our main TV for ten years and we've still got it upstairs.

BLOG POST FROM SEPTEMBER 23 2011 - THE FLOOD

I've never said there aren't some serious upsides to having special needs daughters. I believe I have mentioned previously that the council built an extension to our house to allow the girls to have separate bedrooms. The additional bedroom was built upstairs so, underneath, they also added a playroom for the girls to have their own recreational space, a utility room for the endless washing that the girls create, and also a second bathroom.

The bathroom is where I'm focusing today, because the bathroom made a crucial change in our lives. Yes, having a second bathroom is always handy, but it's the design of the bathroom that is of particular interest here. I believe the term they use is a 'wetroom'. There is a toilet, a sink and a shower in the wetroom, but the shower does not have a cubicle or a door of any kind; the water just falls straight onto the floor. Of course, the floor is covered in some sort of plastic that meets the tiles which start from about six inches up the wall. Not to put too fine a point on it, the room is waterproof. The girls can go and get showered and make all the splashing they like without doing any damage to the house. The shower and the toilet are both built into the wall, so there is a minimum of buttons for them to mess with and cause havoc. The shower itself was very expensive and quite technological. Plus, the lack of cubicle means the person super-vising them has easy access to help them get cleaned, as they are not cocooned in a bath or cubicle. Things weren't always this simple...

The wetroom saved us an awful lot of water troubles

Prior to the arrival of the wetroom, we showered the girls

upstairs in the shower that was in the bath. The girls love playing in water. They like going swimming, playing in the paddling pool, jumping through the sprinkler in the garden, paddling in the river, you name it. Show Libby a two foot wide, one inch deep puddle and she's immediately pulling her shoes and socks off in order to dance about in it.

Bath time, then, was fun time for the girls. The shower was a much better option than the bath for us, though. When Robyn had a bath she would sit on the back edge and push herself off it to slide into the bath, creating a minor tsunami upstairs that flooded the bathroom floor. However, they managed to get water everywhere whatever method we used to wash them. Regularly, you might be sitting at the table in our dining room, eating your dinner or doing some work, minding your own business, when suddenly you would be drenched by a deluge of water. The girls would get water all over the bathroom floor, inches deep, which would seep through the lino, onto the floorboards and through the ceiling until it was running onto the heads of the people downstairs. Then it was all hands to the pump to get as many pans and towels as you could to catch the water so we weren't flooded downstairs, too. The water would run through the cracks that had appeared in the ceiling in the middle of the room, as well as down the walls. This was not a once in a blue moon event like climbing on the roof; this began to happen all the damn time.

A friend of ours recalls a time she visited our home. She was sitting at the dining room table, talking to Karen, when water suddenly came cascading down the wall next to where they were sitting. This had happened many, many times by this stage, so Karen glanced at it and casually grabbed a towel to catch the water. She then just carried on with her conversation, water continuing to flow down the wall, as if nothing even remotely unusual was happening. Our friend sat there agog as the house was flooded. She knew that if this was happening in her house it would be a major catastrophe and people would be running around in a panic. Karen had barely given the situation a second glance. It goes without saying that when we had the extension built, we also had plasterers in to re-plaster the ceiling in the dining room.

Of course, the girls still find ways of causing trouble. Because the danger of flooding or drowning has been eliminated with the wetroom, we are happy to leave the girls to play in the shower for a while before we wash their hair. Libby likes to put the plug in the handbasin and fill it up till it overflows with water, just because she can. She also likes to sneak a plastic sandwich bag and a toy fish into shower time. She then puts the fish in the bag and fills it with water so she can act out scenes from 'Finding Nemo'. It's not unusual to find her in the bathroom at shower time pretending to be the character of the little girl Darla, banging the fish up and down in her bag of water whilst shouting at it, 'Why are you sleeping!!'

And there is one other thing that we have to look out for. We thought we could never have a flood again with the advent of the wetroom, but Robyn will always find a way to get round your best laid plans. Not long after the wetroom had been built, I returned to the shower, having left her in there for a short while, to find water lapping under the playroom door. She had managed to flood the bathroom and the utility room so it was all a good inch deep in water, simply by lying on the bathroom floor on her back and covering up the plughole. Thousands of pounds spent on building a technological solution to our bathing issues in order to create a safe and disaster free environment, all circumvented by Robyn's bum. She's a genius.

6

POOR UNFORTUNATE SOULS - DISNEYLAND PARIS TRIP

PRESENT DAY

Although these posts about our trip to Disneyland Paris were put online in 2011, they were actually written a good few years before then. This, in fact, was where the whole idea of writing a book started, as I sat down and wrote what turned out to be a fairly lengthy account of this 'holiday'. For readers of the blog from back in the day, the story of this family trip is the stuff of legend.

Back in 2005, we planned the trip with our wonderful friends Kate & Spike. George was the oldest at 9, Kate & Spike's boy Elliot was 3 and a half. Four adults, four kids, the girls can get passes so we can all jump the queues, everyone loves Disney... what can possibly go wrong?

Oh boy...

BLOG POST FROM MAY 6 2011 - DISNEYLAND PART I: WISHING (IF I HAD A PHOTOGRAPH OF YOU)

If you know a child with autism, and you know them well, you will most likely know their obsession. You might think I'm making an assumption here, that every child with autism has an obsession, and I suppose I am. But it's a risk I'm willing to take. Autistic kids get obsessed with stuff; it's part of the gig. Obsessions are, if you like, a very common symptom of autism. Lots of boys with autism are fascinated with Thomas the Tank Engine, for instance. My daughters are all about the Disney.

Their various Disney obsessions could easily be an entire posting on its own, but it's sufficient to say here that they love Disney films, Disney characters, Disney toys, Disney clothes... you get the picture. From a young age they have shown their interest, and it's entirely fair to suggest that the spike in the Disney share price in the early part of this century was mostly down to our family's investment in Disney products.

It had been suggested on many occasions that a trip to Disneyland with the girls was a fantastic idea. An idea suggested mostly, it should be noted, by people who were not going to have to actually go with them. We had toyed with the idea for quite a while, wanting to give our daughters the opportunity of a lifetime, knowing in our heart of hearts that there was every possibility that it could end up being a complete disaster. But surely, a place such as Disneyland, a place that is so magical for any young child, would be doubly so for our autistic offspring, right?

The clincher was when our best friends agreed to take the trip with us. Kate & Spike have a son named Elliot who was three at the time, so with four adults and four kids making the journey (obviously our son George was coming, too), it seemed that our long dreamed of trip could finally come true. Spike and I went to the travel agent and booked a trip for eight to Disneyland Paris for October 2005. George was 9, Robyn was 7 and Liberty was 5. It was the perfect time for us to go, and going with friends would mean the perfect solution to the difficulties we might have with Robyn and Libby. The two extra pairs of hands would make all the difference.

Still, there was plenty to get ready before we could even contemplate getting on a plane. For a start, we had to organise three new passports (one each for Karen, Robyn and Libby), a little venture that nearly doubled the cost of the trip. And of course, before you can get a passport, you need a passport quality photo. Have you read the stipulations on how you can pose for passport pictures lately?

- No shadows
- You must face forwards, looking straight towards the camera
- A neutral expression, with your mouth closed (no obvious grinning, frowning or raised eyebrows)
- Your eyes open and clearly visible

Not exactly the easiest set of guidelines for many of us, but we were talking about a 5 year old Libby meeting these requirements. In her younger days, Liberty was far less compliant and we couldn't get her to sit still for five seconds. Plus, if you were to put a camera in front of her, she would immediately start gurning in the most un-passport-picture-like fashion imaginable. Today we would still have a problem, but in a different way. Libby loves to have her photo taken these days, but years of people saying 'Smile!' to her every time they pull a camera out has taken its toll. Try to take a picture of her now and she immediately puts on the most ridiculous ear to ear grin that makes her resemble The Joker after being told the world's funniest joke. You **can** get a good picture of Liberty now, but you have to catch her when she's not paying proper attention.

Still, they weren't likely to let us fly to France without a passport for our kids (they're funny like that about these things) so, one way or another, we had to get some appropriate pictures of our daughters. First of all we tried your standard passport photo booth at a local supermarket. The modern photo machines are better than the ones they had when I was a kid. Back then, you had to brace yourself four times whilst the camera flashed, trying to keep the same pose for each shot. Well, that's not quite right, is it? You would normally try to keep the same pose for three photos; only a heartless mother would deny you the opportunity to pull a 'hilarious' face for the last one. Then you could take it to school the next day and entertain your mates with your 'hysterical' photo. Instead, advances in technology mean that today they will take your picture, show it to you on a screen and, if you approve of the photo, it will print out four identical copies of the same shot. A great idea, especially when you need more than one copy for your passport. Much better than the old days when, despite the fact that you thought you looked great on all the photos, you would find your strip of photos contained one photo that was just about useable, two that had caught you perfectly mid-blink, and one whole-hearted regret that you had elected to pull out your ears and stick your tongue up your nose on the last one.

Well, even with such a brilliant new fangled system, you don't have to be a genius to figure out that none of Robyn or Libby's photos came close to reaching the required standard demanded by the passport office. Eventually, the photo machine gets bored with you telling it you don't like the picture every time one of the girls pulls an inappropriate face, and they print off your fifth attempt whether you like it or not. So, waving goodbye to eight quid, we pondered our next move. A friend told us that if you went to a local photo developing shop, they would take your photo on a digital camera against a blank backdrop and print your picture off there and then. This seemed like a plan; so we headed off there one Saturday morning, just a few short weeks before we were due to go to Disneyland.

I'm not entirely sure what I was expecting at our local Max Spielman shop, but what happened certainly wasn't it. I suppose I'd vaguely hoped that they might take us into a backroom to take our photos in some sort of studio. What actually happens is this: they stand you in the middle of what is a fairly small shop floor, pull down a white blind from the ceiling to act as a plain backdrop, ask you to stand in front of it, and then they take your picture whilst your fellow shoppers all stand gawping at you. I'm sure Karen felt more than a bit self-conscious having her picture taken like that in public, but she quickly got the required shot of herself and we focused our attention on getting some useable pictures of the girls. I held Robyn in place while the shop assistant took a few snaps that were of sufficient quality.

Meanwhile, the good people of Wrexham were having to contend with Liberty, who had decided that Max Spielman wasn't much cop and was doing her best to make a break for the toy shop. Karen and George chased Libby over counters and under displays whilst she squealed the place down. Having caught our increasingly hysterical child, we were then supposed to get her sufficiently settled to get a photograph adhering to stringent passport standards. Perhaps someone could send this challenge to Tom Cruise as a plot idea for the next Mission: Impossible film.

We were in trouble. We were due to go on holiday in a couple of weeks and we didn't have a photo of Liberty that came even close to meeting the necessary criteria for a passport. The trip to Disneyland Paris was all booked, but without a passport for Libby we wouldn't be going anywhere. We tried to take snaps at home with a digital camera, but you might recall that digital cameras in the early days invariably had a time delay between the time of pressing the button and when the picture was actually taken. If you were lucky enough to get Libby sitting still long *enough to take a picture, by the time the flash went off she was already looking the other way.*

As luck would have it, someone heard of our plight who happened to have a very expensive Nikon DSLR camera that took photos without the time delay. They came around to our house, fully prepared for the long haul, but hoping that we might get just one crucial picture for the passport. Then, Liberty produced one of those frustratingly wonderful moments that autism can bring into your life. We perched her on the sideboard, called her attention to the camera and hoped for the best. It was at this very moment that Libby decided to become a child model. She sat there, looking directly at the camera, not pulling any silly faces but with the merest hint of a smile. The camera flashed away, and within half a minute we had a dozen perfectly acceptable photos to choose from. It's easy when you know how.

Libby dressed in her Disney Princess coat with
umbrella on Christmas Morning 2004

BLOG POST FROM MAY 13 2011 - DISNEYLAND PART II: LEARNING TO FLY

Our entire trip to Disneyland was planned with the understanding that our friends Kate & Spike would be going with us. They would be able to help us with the girls and make the difficult moments more bearable. And, of course, it would just be so much more fun and enjoyable to go with friends. It should be stressed that it was only on this proviso that we agreed to even entertain the idea of going to Disneyland Paris with our children.

Now, it's fair to say that I'm always a little sceptical when I read autobiographical accounts and people remember exact details of conversations. It's easy to pretend you remember something that you really don't, or imagine you had a bad feeling about an event before it happened. But I do remember the phone ringing on the morning that we were due to leave, and Karen answering the phone at the top of the stairs. Maybe I picked up on something in Karen's voice as she started to speak to Kate, but I swear that I instantly knew that something bad had happened and our friends would not be coming to Paris with us. This is a blog about my family and not anyone else's, so it is sufficient to say that Kate was unwell, would need to go to hospital and we were worried about her.

What were we to do? Should we stay or should we go? It was an awful decision to have to make. We had no desire to go to Disneyland without our friends for so many reasons. We also felt it would be heartless to swan off on holiday leaving our friend recovering in hospital. Having said that, we knew that Kate & Spike had lots of family close by; it wouldn't be a case of them needing us. In fact, we knew them well enough to know that they would feel guilty for stopping us going, and they had much more important things to worry about than that.

I remember that we were undecided about what to do all day. In fact, about an hour before we were due to leave, Karen and I decided not to go. But then, someone changed our minds: George. We felt sure our autistic daughters would love Disneyland, but they had no concept of us taking a trip there. If we didn't go, they wouldn't be upset because they didn't really understand that we were going in the first place. However, George was nine years-old in 2005 and had been looking forward to going to Disneyland for months. The lot of a sibling of autistic children can be a miserable one at times. One of the most trying things for parents of a family with autistic and non-autistic children is trying to find a balance between caring for those that need 'special' attention, and ensuring the others know that they are special, too. To just ditch the trip to Disneyland, minutes before we were due to leave, would have been devastating for any young child, including George. Going to Paris was the right thing to do, but it was a trip we were undertaking with two adult pairs of hands instead of four as we had planned all along. Karen and I knew that we were now in for a hell of a ride – and I'm not talking about Space Mountain.

WHEN GETTING READY TO TAKE CHILDREN WITH AUTISM TO THE AIRPORT to board a plane, you must thoroughly prepare. That's right; make sure you have all your children's favourite treats, drinks, toys and books. Indeed, prepare yourself by taking anything that will help occupy your children in this autism unfriendly environment. Then, most importantly of all, prepare yourself for the fact that all of your preparations will not be nearly enough and you are about to experience the most hellish couple of hours of your life.

Obviously, you'd like to spend as little time at the airport as possible, but you can't turn up to the check-in too late or you won't get to sit together on the plane. When we arrived, Karen went and stood in the check-in line whilst George and I tried to keep Robyn and Liberty entertained. A few days before, we had wisely gone up to the airport to undertake a recce. We discovered that there was one thing the girls loved about the airport; the travelators. I have always wondered why when humans step into airports we apparently lose the ability to walk, but mankind's laziness was, in this situation, autism's gain.

The girls ran up and down the travelators to their hearts' content, and when they were done running up and down they would just lie down and travel along on their backs, staring at the ceiling as they were carried along. We had to shout for them to quickly get up when they approached the end so their hair didn't get pulled under resulting in a catastrophic accident, but other than that it was an entirely suitable way of passing the time. The workers at the airport were less impressed, and it almost goes without saying that we got all manner of filthy looks from our fellow travellers as the girls ran screaming about the place. Part of you wants to explain to them why they are acting this way, and another part of you doesn't really see why you should need to. It's this part of me that usually wins out, and I just walk away quietly cursing the judgmental idiots. Of course, this is completely unfair. Would I think terribly differently if I saw someone else's kids playing merry hell at the airport? Probably not, though I hope I would be able to keep my opinions to myself.

George and I had to check back every now and again to see if Karen had made it to the front of the queue. When she did, I had to try and check in, signing forms and writing on tags whilst I put Robyn in the only place I could keep her under control; on my shoulders. Putting the girls on your shoulders is a winner in these situations; they love being up high and they can't run off. Robyn was still trying to escape while she was up there, but we managed to get the job done.

The real low was when we had to go through the x-ray security doorways. We approached with Robyn on my shoulders and Liberty on Karen's. We all stopped and put our wallets and keys in the trays, but the girls had to get off our shoulders at this point to go sensibly through the portal. This was the moment the girls had been waiting for and they seized it. They both hurtled under the security rope and around the doorway, rather than through it, screaming at the top of their voices as they went. Our natural instinct was to chase after them, but several burly airport security types prevented us both from doing so.

This time we did try to explain the situation, and some official looking airport employees tried to tell the girls to go back to the other side of the security gate. Of course, the girls didn't understand a word. It was beyond awkward as we tried to give the people chasing our daughters a lesson on how to deal with autistic children by shouting across an airport security area, and the staff didn't look the least bit impressed. Just a quick aside for any potential terrorists who may have felt the need to dip their toe into my blog this week: if you're thinking of using special needs kids in a cunning plot to get you through airport security without being properly searched, forget it. They really don't care.

We decided to try to be the last to board the plane so Robyn and Libby would be cooped up on board for as short a time as possible. We tried to keep them entertained by having them sit on top of our luggage trolley as we wandered around the terminal, which they quite enjoyed. We were told on a number of occasions by separate airport workers that this method of traversing the airport was forbidden, but we felt that keeping our girls from having a complete meltdown was far more important than kow-towing to the Health & Safety police, so we nodded politely and ignored them. They're just doing their job, but so was I. We had endured two hours of people looking down their noses at us whilst the girls excelled themselves with some of their most inappropriate public behaviour yet. This was just about self-preservation now.

When we finally got onto the plane, there was still a small queue to actually take our seats. Robyn and Liberty decided to *escape our clutches and crawl through other passengers' legs, which meant we had to drop to our knees and pull them back through people's legs, kicking and screaming. Fortunately, the line quickly subsided and we could finally take our seats and get ready to fly to Paris. Surely the worst was behind us now. Right?*

BLOG POST FROM MAY 20 2011 - DISNEYLAND PART III: IN THE AIR TONIGHT

So, having started our trip to Disneyland Paris without any outside help, enduring the living hell of the airport, we were ready for take off.

The first thing we discovered on the plane was that we had failed in our attempt to get seats sitting next to each other. We were actually seated in three different places; had it have been four different places then one of the girls would have been totally unsupervised next to some stranger, which would have been entertaining for someone. When we realised the separation situation, I just knew that we would be sitting next to the kind of people who had been sneering at us since we got to the airport. But, for the first time in twelve hours, we got a little bit lucky.

Nine year-old George sat on his own, but the lady he sat next to seemed very pleasant and chatted kindly to him, which helped put him at ease. At least this wasn't his first time on a plane, as he had been to the States about 18 months previously to see his cousins. Karen sat between Liberty and a lady who had at least heard of autism and seemed very understanding. Meanwhile, I sat with Robyn on one side of me and a very agreeable Scottish businessman on the other. Not only was he a genial fellow, he was the father of a boy with semantic pragmatic disorder, a condition similar to autism in matters of communication. As we both watched Robyn, we swapped stories about our children; the experience was very reassuring after the nerve shredding couple of hours we had just experienced.

In fairness to our girls, it has to be said that, once we got them settled into their seats, they were absolutely fantastic. Here, all of our preparation actually did pay off. Robyn, who quite enjoys travelling, stared with curiosity at everything that was going on outside her window. She has had a number of problems with her ears and we were a bit worried about how she might be affected by the pressure on them at take-off. To our relief, she showed no signs of stress or concern, no doubt helped by her eating several Refresher chew bars (to help her to swallow) which we had kept back until we were ready to take-off. Personal DVD players were the height of technology at the time, and we had borrowed one from a friend. So, once we got going, Robyn fired up Pocahontas with her headphones on and was perfectly happy. Libby sat eating sweets and listening to Disney tunes on my iPod and the flight itself passed without incident. When the flight stewardess asked us to put the DVD player away as we came into land at Paris, the gentleman next to me explained the situation to her and she left us alone.

We were aware that once the plane had come to a stop we needed to get off as soon as possible. You know that really frustrating bit on flights when everyone wants to get off the plane, but you have to wait for everyone to retrieve their luggage before shuffling off the plane at snail's pace? We had to somehow avoid that. Brilliantly, our kind Scottish businessman stood up and stopped anyone getting past while we got all of our luggage and kids together. Whoever you were, sir, we salute you.

Now we were off the plane, the girls were looking to do a runner at the first available opportunity, so we kept them on our shoulders whilst going through passport control. All we needed to do now was quickly find our luggage and find the driver that we had booked to take us on the hour's drive from Charles de Gaulle Airport to Disneyland. However, here our previous good *fortune worked against us. Having got quickly off the plane and avoided incident at passport control, we arrived at the luggage carousels significantly earlier than our luggage. Robyn was still on my shoulders but, even though she was only seven at the time, she's always been a tall girl and, at this stage, seemed to weigh several metric tonnes. In any case, even Robyn gets bored of being on your shoulders after a while. So, we let the girls get down, and George and I had to try to keep the girls from going too wild, whilst Karen kept an eye on the luggage situation. She watched suitcase after suitcase arrive through the black plastic curtain, take their little trip on the conveyor belt, then disappear through the exit before re-appearing again through their original entrance. Eventually, our luggage emerged through the fronds of plastic. In our haste to get our cases onto our trolley, we made a teeny-tiny-but-oh-so-crucial mistake. We took our eyes off the girls for less than ten seconds.*

As I put the last suitcase onto our trolley I felt an urgent tap on my shoulder. I turned around to find a man pointing in the direction of the carousel as he said, 'Is that your daughter?' I looked to see Robyn, not only riding the carousel, but about to disappear through the exit for the luggage. I leapt into action, boarding the moving conveyor at speed and diving to drag Robyn back before she disappeared beyond the black plastic curtain. But I was too late; she had already gone through. I paused momentarily, but realised I had no choice but to follow her.

I don't know what I was expecting to find, but I think I was slightly disappointed to find a road, a skip full of luggage, and several slightly bemused Frenchmen staring at me, no doubt wondering what the hell I was doing there. They were putting the luggage onto a strip of the conveyor belt that went along the outside to go through to where the luggage emerged for the passengers to claim.

I quickly grabbed hold of Robyn and managed to bundle her

back through the exit hole, whilst Karen dragged her back from the other side. I was about to follow her to make a similar re-entry, but the airport workers prevented me with excited shouts of, 'Non! Non!' whilst pointing further along the conveyor belt. They clearly wanted me to use a different entrance further along. I walked to where they were pointing, expecting to find a door for me to enter back into the airport. It quickly became clear that there was no such door; the only entrance back into the airport was the very entrance used by the luggage. There was no alternative. I clambered aboard the conveyor belt, sitting cross-legged between a couple of suitcases so I could fit through the small entrance, hoping there wouldn't be anyone standing there to see me squeezed onto the carousel like a piece of luggage. There must have been several planes arriving at this terminal at the same time, because there was an impressive crowd to greet me as I emerged through the entrance with the luggage, and a huge roar of laughter went up from the assembled gathering. I gave a jaunty salute of acknowledgement and hauled myself off the carousel. I can imagine that it was a funny sight to see, standing waiting for your luggage thinking; 'Blue suitcase, red suitcase, rucksack, grown man sitting cross-legged...' Embarrassing? A little. But, I think, of all the tales of Robyn's expeditions I have to tell, this one has been aired the most.

Next, we went to meet our driver who was going to drive us to the resort. As we exited the baggage area, there were lots of drivers standing holding signs with names on. We searched for one with 'Dickenson' on, but there wasn't one to be found. I pushed the trolley with Robyn on top of the luggage, whilst Karen held Liberty's hand. We looked around for quite a while, but we couldn't find our driver anywhere. We dug into our envelope of documents and discovered that we couldn't find any of the literature that related to our shuttle service, for which we had already paid. In desperation, we called my Dad at home to *quickly look up the name of the company he had recommended to us. Armed with this information, we then went to the service desk, but the gentleman there claimed to have never heard of the company we were supposed to be travelling with. Brilliant.*

When I was a kid, my parents always seemed to have things worked out. No matter how much difficulty we were in, I never thought to worry. Mum and Dad were on the case; they'd sort it out. Grown ups know how to do stuff like this, don't they? Clearly, my son, George, has not lived with such security in his life. As I looked at the tears rolling down his cheeks, I knew what we had unwittingly telegraphed to him: 'We are stuck in an airport in Paris, it is almost midnight, the girls are about to lose it, and my Mum and Dad haven't the first clue how we are going to get to Disneyland.' As silent prayers were said, a tiny miracle happened. After about half an hour of looking, now carrying three crying children, Karen stumbled across our driver. He didn't have a sign, but had been looking out for a party with four adults and four kids, which, of course, is what we should have been. In all the commotion, no one had even thought to alert the shuttle company about the change in plan.

We climbed into the small mini-bus, cuddling the girls and reassuring George that everything would be alright now. We documented the trip on a camcorder (though the footage is now lost) and the family members who can talk addressed the camera to talk about our trip so far. What came across in that two minutes of film is the sheer relief to be out of a public place for the first time in six hours, and finally be on our way to Disneyland. Now we could start enjoying our holiday, couldn't we?

BLOG POST FROM MAY 26 2011 - DISNEYLAND PART IV: LIFE IS A ROLLERCOASTER

We arrived at the Sequoia Lodge at Disneyland Paris at around 1am. Thankfully, there was no-one else around in the lobby of the hotel at that time of the morning, so checking-in was fairly pain-less, although Robyn was getting a little upset and restless at having to hang around in an unfamiliar place while Karen filled in the various arrival forms. Quite what we would have done if we'd arrived at peak time with lots of other people and had to queue, I have no idea; but with the girls having now been awake for 21 hours, it would not have been pretty.

The first thing we did when we got to our room was to call Spike to see how Kate was. He assured us that, although she was still in hospital, she was going to be fine. We were relieved to hear it. The only possible upside to not having travelled with our friends was that we still had the two rooms we had booked; there was certainly plenty of space. We had two adjoining rooms that had a door in each room that linked to the other one with a small gap in between; you may have seen that kind of setup in hotels. Normally, occupants would keep these doors locked to prevent intruders from the neighbouring room, but we kept them open to allow the kids to wander between the rooms and have more space. It also meant that we had four double beds to share between five of us, so three of us had a double bed each, and Liberty and I shared.

Following a decent night's sleep, we started to get ready to experience the excitement of Disneyland. However, as we got ready, we found that the locks on the main doors might be suffi-cient to keep other people out, but, as you should know by now, our security concerns are all about keeping certain people in. The locks were simply a knob that turned 180 degrees. Maybe a very young child might not be able to figure this out, but there's a reason we have number locks on every internal door in our house; these things weren't going to even come close to doing the job of foiling the escapades of our freedom loving daugh-ters. I lost count of the number of times Robyn escaped and went roaming the corridors. These huge hotels are like a maze, and it doesn't require much imagination to envisage Robyn getting herself into big trouble with Libby tagging along to help out.

On one occasion, Liberty went into the adjoining room whilst the rest of us were trying to relax. Whilst pottering about, she managed to lock the front door of the other room, preventing entrance from the corridor; she then closed the adjoining door and locked that as well. She was now completely locked in, and though we shouted for her to unlock the door, we may as well have been shouting for her to whip up a chicken carbonara with the contents of her bag of Monster Munch; Libby can only understand the simplest of commands at the best of times. She started to get upset that she was stuck on her own, highlighting a big difference between her and Robyn; you get the feeling sometimes that if Robyn could manage to lock the entire world out of the room she was occupying, she absolutely would. Before the situation became a real crisis, Libby inadvertently unlocked the front door and George was able to enter the room from the corridor.

Eventually, we realised that the only way we could be in the hotel room without major trauma was for us both to be on full time security patrol. There was a main exit to both rooms, so that meant that two parents had to sit on the floor with their backs to each door to prevent any escape. To while away the time, Karen and I would shout conversations to each other in the adjoining room. When we got home and people asked us how our 'holiday' to Disneyland went, it was difficult to just be pleasant and say 'lovely' in any sort of believable way.

When we had finally got the kids ready, we headed out to the Disneyland Park itself, which was within walking distance from our hotel. I expected the girls to be bowled over by what they saw, but I should have known better than to think I would get a predictable response from my daughters. On the lost home video footage that we had, there was an interesting scene of us walking over to the Park for the first time.

Before you get there you walk through Disney Village. This is basically a street full of Disney themed shops, designed to fleece you of your hard-earned before you even get on your first ride. But, Disney didn't get where they are today without being able to make the mundane seem rather exciting, and Disney Village does just that. However, Robyn wasn't interested in the wonderland around her at all. Robyn had found something far more interesting to monopolise her attention: a waterfall. Actually, to call it a waterfall is being extremely charitable. It was a dribble of water emerging from a hole in a yellow brick wall, but Robyn stood for a long, long time, sipping at a Pepsi, unable to take her eyes off it. At moments like these, I don't think it's entirely unreasonable to glance at the Disney treasure trove surrounding you, look again at your child, transfixed by a miserable few litres of water trundling down a wall, and mentally calculate how much you are spending for them to be there (financially and emotionally), watching something less impressive than you could conjure up at your own kitchen sink.

George and me, with Robyn on my shoulders as we
head into the Disney Village

There was one major upside to our family situation, and we had planned ahead to take full advantage of it. We took our daughters' educational statements, but also a letter for each girl from the school doctor. These letters not only confirmed their diagnosis, but stated categorically that there was no way Robyn or Libby could do any queuing at the park. Nice work, Doc! Carrying all our documentation, we headed straight for the Disney 'Town Hall' (an information centre), to get our special pass. It may well have been the case that the Disney 'hosts' would only have needed to spend two minutes in the girls' company to know they had special needs, but having all our documentation certainly meant that it was a 'no questions asked' deal.

The camcorder footage we had showed George filming us as we walked away from our first ride. Far from being stressed and frustrated, my tone came across as something approaching triumphant. We were given a blue form that was our proof of the girls' additional needs, and told to go to the exit for the ride, rather than the entrance. We would then be met by one of the impeccably trained staff who would ask us to wait a minute or two whilst they reserved a car for us. Then we climbed in, and we were off. The line for the Peter Pan ride, which was the first we went to, must have been easily over an hour. For us to be able to waltz past the entire queue, show our pass, take the ride, get off again, having the whole thing done in about five minutes, was nothing short of fantastic. For once, for all of us, our girls' issues were an unqualified bonus, rather than the nightmares we had been experiencing for the last sixteen hours, and for most of the five years previous. The great thing was, we had exactly the same agreement for every attraction we took our daughters to. We were now part of the Mickey Mouse Club (Autism Division), and membership certainly had its privileges.

Unfortunately, for Robyn and Liberty, sometimes not even this privileged method of experiencing Disneyland was good enough. There were a number of occasions when our two to three minute wait to board the ride resulted in an almighty melt-down from one or both of the girls. We did our best to explain to the girls that we would be on the ride 'in a minute', but all they could see was a fantastic attraction going on right in front of them, and we were stopping them from experiencing it. Although the girls have improved hugely in this regard as they have aged, waiting their turn was a concept they couldn't begin to get their heads around at the ages of 5 and 7. I have to admit that, some-what unusually, I found these outbursts a little embarrassing. Not the tantrum itself, (goodness knows we've experienced enough public fireworks to be pretty much immune to shame in these situations), but the fact that they were going **so** nuts, when they only had to wait **two minutes**, whilst other kids were patiently waiting **hours** for their turn. I just wished that I could have been able to make them understand how short their waiting time was, just to help them calm down. Two minutes waiting time for something so good really wasn't worth them getting so upset.

When you weigh up all the difficult experiences the girls have, and the knock-on effect they have on the other members of the family, it's not such a huge deal to be able to skip to the front of the line at a theme park, is it? But, believe me; it makes an impossible trip just about bearable.

BLOG POST FROM MAY 29 2011 - DISNEYLAND PART V: HOME AND DRY

On TV ads for Disneyland, you always see kids milling around with Mickey Mouse, Snow White and all their Disney pals. In fair-ness to Disney, these guys are knocking about the park throughout the day, and you can meet them and have your picture taken. Unfortunately, whenever we saw any of the char-acters, there were seemingly thousands of kids and their parents waiting to meet them, and it was unlikely that our blue paper queue jumper pass was going to cut much ice here.

Miraculously though, whilst walking down Main Street on our final afternoon in the park, Minnie Mouse seemed to just appear right in front of us. People almost instantly flocked around her like flies on a cowpat, and whilst we were quickly bundled out of the way by the baying hordes, Libby still found herself standing right next to Minnie herself. A big crowd of people now separated us from Libby, so while other kids were waiting to have their picture taken, Libby was busy tweaking Minnie's nose and putting her head up her skirt. Like you do. We had to fight our way through the crowds to rescue our daughter, also preventing her from further assaulting one of the world's best loved cartoon characters. I very much doubt that even Mickey has had the intimate access to Minnie Mouse that Liberty has.

A different problem that we had at Disneyland was the issue of food. We took all of Robyn's favourite crisps and treats with us, but she wouldn't entertain the idea of eating them. No matter how often we drew her attention to her favourite flavour Monster Munch, she just pushed our hands away. The only thing she ate the entire time we were away was McDonald's cheeseburgers. How do McDonald's do it? Whoever does their advertising is a marketing genius. My daughters are oblivious to an awful lot that goes on around them, but try driving past the golden arches without stopping and they'll burst into tears. And how do they make their campaigns so appealing, so attractive, that a kid whose diet basically consists of curry flavoured mushrooms still eats double cheeseburgers like they are the last food on earth?

By the second day, Robyn had eaten so little that I bought her six cheeseburgers for lunch. She immediately sussed out that they must use slightly different flour for the buns in French McDonald's, because she wouldn't touch them. Nobody else could tell the difference, but then a lot of people can't tell the difference between Coke and Pepsi, and we know a little lady who certainly can. So she sat there, good as gold, wolfing down six of those 100% real beef patties (apparently), coated with their slices of processed cheese. She would have eaten more, but I ordered ten, thinking that was a bit over the top, and Libby had already eaten four.

Quite why she wouldn't eat crisps or sugar puffs or sweets or any of the other snacks she enjoyed at that time, I honestly don't know. I appreciate that we were in a very different environment to home, but I would have thought that she would have wanted things from home to impose her own routine on her new surroundings. It clearly doesn't work that way.

At the end of the second day we returned to the hotel to pick up our luggage and board the bus to the airport. I think it's some-thing of an understatement to say that Karen and I were really looking forward to getting home. We collected our luggage and Karen took the girls off to get them changed into their pyjamas so they would be comfortable on the plane. These had been put in our carry-on case to make the transition as seamless as possi-ble. We really had thought all this through. Then we put our suit-cases on the pavement outside the hotel and tried to wait for the bus whilst preventing Robyn and Libby from doing a runner. Just as we were expecting the bus to arrive, Karen went into our hand luggage to dig out the envelope that contained all of our tickets for the coach and the plane. They weren't there.

You must have been in these situations. You try to remain calm and look again and again, telling yourself that they are there, and if you just look for the seventeenth time, they will appear this time – but they didn't. The bus to the airport came and went without us. We went back into the hotel and spoke to the concierge who found a room for Karen to go into to unpack our entire luggage. That left me with three children in a hotel lobby, two of whom were extremely restless. They'd spent the last two days tazzing around on rollercoasters and aero-planes; sitting still and being good in a public place just wasn't on their list of 'Things to Do at Disneyland'.

Robyn was squealing and running off in one direction, Liberty *was desperate to take a ride in the elevators that were in another direction, so I put Robyn on my shoulders and tried to drag Liberty away from the lifts with my free hand. As Liberty is wont to do when she is being deprived of something, she point blank refused to walk. So when I say I dragged her around the hotel lobby, that's exactly what I mean. George was trying his best to help, but he was in tears again. 'Mum and Dad are quite obviously useless and I am going to be stuck in France forever', he said. Alright, he didn't actually say that, but he didn't need to. Or perhaps he was just cursing the rotten luck we were having on this trip on top of everything else. I know I was.*

After what seemed an eternity (do we enter a different way of measuring time when we've been left alone with a bunch of fractious kids? It always seems a lot longer than traditional watches actually tell us it is), a smiling Karen emerged, tearfully grasping the tickets. Though we have no idea how, the tickets had managed to find their way to the bottom of the last suitcase Karen checked. After many 'merci beaucoups' to the concierge, we went to catch the next coach, which would hopefully still get us to the airport on time.

Checking in at Charles de Gaulle was as much fun as it had been at Manchester. Yet again, Karen joined the queue whilst George and I did our best to entertain Robyn and Liberty on the travelators. Only, by now, the travelators had rather lost their charm. This was understandable; the girls had spent the last two days on Thunder Mountain and Pirates of the Caribbean – trundling along at walking pace on a flat track was pretty small fry in comparison. Libby, in particular, wasn't playing ball. I have one very strong memory of walking down the concourse, holding Robyn's hand on my left and literally dragging a screaming Libby along the floor by her reigns with my right hand. My, how the Parisian travellers who passed us by were impressed with my parenting skills.

Eventually, we got to the departure lounge. Here there was a pair of escalators to take you from the lounge area to the shops and restaurants which Robyn tore up and down for half an hour whilst I did my best to follow her. This wasn't easy; when people held up her progress she just slipped through their legs, which I suppose I could have done, but, you know, I didn't. In the lounge itself she had placed a bag of Monster Munch perfectly in the middle of the floor between the two sets of seats. Anytime anyone touched it she darted back to make sure it was at perfect mathematical right angles with its environment. Over-zealous cleaners tried to clear the Monster Munch away on several occasions, and were greeted with an almighty paddy from Robyn for their troubles.

The girls obviously knew that we were waiting to get on a plane, because when we boarded a bus to take a short ride to the plane itself, they went absolutely bananas; it was all we could do to keep them on the bus. Robyn kept throwing herself at the doors to get out. It was a little like waiting a short time to get on the rides back at the park, except it seemed she was so anxious to get on a plane she was willing to throw herself to a premature death by exiting a moving bus.

We eventually boarded the plane, walking up the steps from the tarmac. This was something I hadn't done before, and I'm sure the girls enjoyed seeing the monstrous jet they were boarding at close quarters. Again, once they were on the plane, the girls were fabulous. There were two rows of three seats across the plane and we took up a row between the five of us. No separation this time, and we even had a spare seat on which to put some of the items we needed for the girls. Libby and I sat together, and she amused herself by listening to Disney tunes on her iPod and playing with a Cinderella toy we had bought her that spun around and lit up in bright colours when a button was pressed. A short time before we touched down in Manchester, Libby fell asleep. I know it sounds a little over-sentimental, but I remember watching her, lying on my arm, her eyes *slowly closing, clutching Cinderella, and thinking she looked like an angel. Liberty is so beautiful when she's asleep.*

Finally, we were home. Kate was now home from hospital and recovering well, so Spike picked us up from the airport. We piled into the car and headed back to Wrexham, but there was time for just one more piece of drama. As we sped along the M53, Spike's BMW had a tyre blowout. We quickly pulled over to change the tyre, but this proved more difficult than we had anticipated. We had managed to have the blowout on a section of motorway completely devoid of any lighting. It was 11pm, late October, and pitch black. Spike searched his car for a torch he thought might be there, but he was mistaken. Then Karen had a lifesaving brainwave and retrieved an item from our hand luggage that could provide a light source so we could actually see the tyre to change it. So, there we were, enjoying one final surreal moment, changing a car tyre on the hard shoulder of the M53 in the middle of the night, aided by light provided by a spinning multicoloured Cinderella toy. It had been that kind of holiday.

Karen helps Spike to change the tyre with a little help
from Cinderella

The morning after, feeling very relieved to be home, we sat

on our settee and took stock of our experience. Liberty kept coming up to us and whispering, 'Disneyland Paris', in the manner she had seen in so many TV commercials; so she seemed to have enjoyed herself. When Robyn, who had been unsettled the whole time we were away, dashed around the house, stuffing herself with crisps and laughing her head off, clearly thrilled to be back in familiar surroundings... well, we didn't know whether to laugh or cry. She does look at the photos and smile sometimes, so she must have enjoyed some of it, though I suspect it was mostly the time she actually spent on the rides. Robyn does love her theme park rides.

All in all, we must have spent around £1500 on our two day trip, which is a lot of money for a single-income family, especially when that single income comes from teaching. George quite enjoyed some of the trip, apart from the frequent traumas (and there were many other slightly less exciting but nerve fraying experiences I haven't told you about), and the girls enjoyed the odd moment here and there. Karen and I rarely remember the experience without shuddering. Would we go again? Almost certainly not. Am I sorry we did it? Well, when I see Robyn flicking through the holiday photos and smiling, it pleases me. And it was a really memorable experience for all of us on so many levels. And I'm glad that we tried a holiday with the girls, because at least we know what it's actually like now. And we'll always remember Robyn and Liberty grinning whilst zooming around Thunder Mountain, and their Dad arriving with the luggage on the airport carousel.

Yes, we'll always have Paris.

George, Robyn, Dad and Libby getting ready to enter
the Disneyland park

PRESENT DAY

Well, that was 2005. It's now 2021 and we haven't been on a family holiday since. George went on holidays with either one of his parents, with his grandparents and even, as he got older, by himself. But the five of us together? No. A day out was the most we ever tried and, even now, those can still be hard work.

But, just recently, Libby has started to whisper about Disneyland Paris once more and, when the pandemic allows, we plan on trying a family holiday to Disneyland again with the girls who are, of course, 21 and 23 these days. Obviously, we are much more experienced at dealing with these situations now. Robyn, in particular, is very calm and good at waiting these days. And Libby is fantastic as long as nothing bad happens. It should go really well and we will almost certainly have an amazing time.

We're absolutely mad for even considering it, aren't we?

7

CRUEL SUMMER - TRIPS OUT

BLOG POST FROM FEBRUARY 12 2011 - S.H.O.P.P.I.N.G.

D uring the weekends and school holidays, we try to get the girls out of the house at least once a day. If they don't get out at some point, we will usually suffer the consequences. The consequences of cooping the girls up in the house all day... Well, that's at least a blog in itself.

They don't usually need to do anything too exciting. A trip to a play park or a walk in the country for an hour, for instance; this type of trip out will give them the bit of freedom they need to stop them going stir crazy when we get back to the house. However, living in Britain as we do, the weather is not always sufficiently pleasant for us to even go for a walk in our local country park. The 'summer' holiday also means that we can't spend money on entertainment every day, as they are off school for 44 days in a row and we'd soon be broke. Inevitably, from time to time, we think it's a good idea to take them shopping with us. In fairness, as the girls have got older, we do sometimes manage to get through these trips without major trauma. Sometimes.

If we have remembered to take iPads and iPods with us, this

is a definite bonus. But we're not always that organised and, even if we are, it's not a foolproof way of securing a successful shopping trip. First of all, there's the shopping trolley situation. Liberty (aged 10) can just about get in the child seat with a struggle, but Robyn becomes a teenager in a week or two, and that just ain't happening anymore. So, most of the time, Robyn rides in the trolley itself where you put the food. On occasion, we have been accosted by the health and safety police to tell us this is not acceptable. It's quite simple, supermarket guys – provide us with an appropriate trolley with adequate seating for grown special needs kids, or shut the hell up. I promise I won't sue you if Robyn hurts herself by sitting in the trolley (though, given that you've neglected to provide for our needs, maybe I should – that would wake the rapscallions up.)

Costco have the flatbed trolleys which the girls like to
ride around on. The actual food goes in the standard
trolley being pushed by Karen

In fairness, some supermarkets do have trolleys that can be used by older special needs children or adults. Unfortunately, because they tend to be attractive to local hoodlums who like to ride around on them for larks and break them, the staff always lock them up somewhere. This means that in order to actually get to use the special trolleys, we have to queue up at Customer Services, where we usually speak to someone who doesn't know what we are talking about, who has to go and get someone who does know what we're talking about but doesn't know where the keys are, who has to go and find out where the keys are before they can take us back outside to unlock the trolleys, which have been used by other shoppers as rubbish bins and the seats are covered in dirt and dust and have to be cleaned with our hands. All the while this has been going on, the girls just have to stand still waiting and, frankly, the girls don't do standing still and waiting. Faced with this prospect, we often just take our chances with a regular trolley.

So, after all that faff, we finally get into the store. We split the shopping list into two and go off on separate missions with a child each. I always give my wife Karen the choice of Robyn or Liberty, which I think this is a pretty gallant gesture. But, it's like predicting the winning stick in 'pooh sticks', the game where you both drop a stick on one side of the bridge and run over to the other side to see which one emerges first. A stick is a stick; there's nothing about a stick that's really going to tell you which one will be the first under a bridge. And there's no real way of knowing which of the girls is going to behave worse than the other on any given day. You may as well just grab the child nearest to you.

Libby is usually quite demanding. We never get out of Sainsbury's without Libby clutching a slushy from the supermarket cafeteria, but this is a better deal than we used to get. Karen can tell many stories from Libby's pre-school years where she's had to spend £10-15 on a toy because Libby has seen it and refused to leave the store without it. You either splashed the cash or experienced a complete meltdown from our youngest child. Believe me, if you've ever experienced a Libby tantrum, you'd realise that spending a tenner to avoid such a trauma represents excellent value.

The public meltdown can provide some of the real lows of being a parent of children with autism. I've seen Robyn and Liberty go absolutely hysterical for some minor reason or other, and you have to try and deal with it in the full glare of the judgmental public. The difficult thing about this is that the girls' physical appearance is completely 'normal'. Harsh as I know it sounds, some special needs conditions such as Down's Syndrome or Cerebral Palsy make it extremely obvious to the casual observer that this child has additional needs. It is only our girls' behaviour that sets them apart from other kids, so the public tantrum means that everyone is looking at you without any idea that there are additional needs involved. It can be a tough experience.

When Karen took George to America a few years back, I remember taking Robyn shopping with me, and as we were about to leave the store she started using her dragging technique to take me up and down the aisles until we ended up at the Pickled Onion Monster Munch. The thing was, we already had several multipacks of Monster Munch at home. We only live ten minutes from the supermarket, so I could just tell her we've got lots of them at home and she can have as many as she likes when we get back. Robyn can understand that concept, right? Needless to say, we ended up with even more Monster Munch than we needed. When shopping with Robyn and Liberty, it seems you always end up paying a premium just to get out of the supermarket without an experience that sees you losing the will to live.

BLOG POST FROM AUGUST 30 2011 - RAIN IN THE SUMMERTIME

And so, we approach the end of the summer holidays here in Britain. For some of you, 'summer holidays' is simply a reminder of more innocent times gone by when you had a sizeable chunk of the summer months with nothing to do but lark about. For others, it's still a big part of your lives; either because you are still in education, or you have children that are. Your experience of the summer break will hugely affect your feelings as the holidays come to an end. You will either be disappointed or thrilled. As a teacher, I have to return to work in a few days; never a good thing. However, when Karen packs the kids off to school next week, after six weeks without a break, she will be metaphorically punching the air. She may literally punch the air in celebration, I don't know. As I'm at work I'm not there to see what she does when there's no-one around, but a bit of fist pumping in these circumstances would seem reasonable enough.

It seems, then, a good time to reflect on what has happened this summer. The good news is that our summer was fairly uneventful. Uneventful is always good in our house. Uneventful means not having to deal with escapes, roof climbs or the emergency services. I remember the first day of the holidays quite well, though. This summer, we had a fair amount of support for the girls from the local authority through various support outlets, for which we are grateful. However, there are still plenty of days without support, which means finding something for the family to do so the girls don't go stir crazy.

On the first day of the holidays we took a trip out so we could all go for a walk. On our return we decided to call in at Iceland (the frozen food store, rather than the so-called land of fire and ice) to pick up some iced lollies for Liberty and a Magnum for Robyn (so she could, as always, pick all the chocolate off and throw the ice cream away). We took the girls in so that they could choose what they wanted, and Liberty picked up a box of Twisters. She then decided she also wanted a huge bar of chocolate, which wasn't happening as she was already having an ice cream and we had chocolate at home. With a throwback to the bad old days, she threw herself to the ground and started kicking and screaming to the dismay of her parents and our fellow shoppers. I managed to physically remove her from the store and drag her to the car. Her temper continued unabated until someone put a Twister ice cream in her hand, at which point it immediately ceased. Just the way to start 44 days off school with the kids: a meltdown in Iceland.

At a local country park they have a scheme where they hire out specially adapted bicycles for disabled people and their carers. Karen and I took Robyn and Libby one day, and we got three wheelers with two seats alongside each other, rather like the front seats of a car. Both seats have handlebars (though the carer sits behind the set that actually work), there are two sets of pedals slightly in front of you (a bit like a pedalo) so you can both power this heavy vehicle, and there is a gear leaver between the two seats. I took Robyn and we set off on our 'bike' on the walking path around the park. It wasn't too difficult to power this contraption along the flat terrain, and it was a lot of fun going downhill. Robyn giggled with delight as we got some speed together, and that is always something that is lovely to see. However, going up the hills was horrific. There only needed to be the slightest incline and we had to move down into first gear and make a major, major effort to get this hulking beast to move. Of course, at this point, Robyn no longer felt the need to pedal. Why would she pedal uphill? That's hard work! Eventually I had to get off and push the bike uphill while Robyn sat there, smiling at the world going by. The idea that getting off and walking for a bit would make the bike lighter and life a lot easier for her dad never even crossed her mind. It's a lovely life our girls lead.

Robyn getting ready for me to chauffeur her around
the park

Another little activity we do on days off with the girls is to take the car to be washed. Whilst the car gets a more effective clean if it is washed by hand, this is not nearly as fun for the girls as going through an electric car wash where your car is attacked by those big furry monsters. I actually remember thinking this was exciting when I was very small and the girls still really enjoy it. It's funny to watch their faces light up as the rollers close in on the car and squirt water everywhere. As is the case with many situations in life, Libby sees a link to an animated film she likes, in this case the Dreamworks movie Shark Tale. This was the one where Will Smith voices the character of Oscar who works at a car wash. So, in the film, of course, they sing the classic Rose Royce disco tune of the same name. When we've gone through the car wash before, we've had the CD in the car and been able to play it for Libby to sing along while we drove through. This summer we didn't have that CD in the car with us, so Libby made us sing it for her instead. There's always that slight worry that the people operating the machinery will hear two grown adults singing Car Wash rather excitedly and wonder what sad acts would do such a thing but, to be honest, we got past the stage of being embarrassed with our kids years ago.

An encouraging development this summer saw our local cinema stage a showing of a film specifically for children with autism. They had brighter lighting, the sound levels reduced, and the kids were free to wander around if they wished, knowing that other parents and customers would not be judging them. We did not have Libby on the day it was on as she was at a care centre for children with autism. We told the workers at the centre about it, though, and they took all the kids along for that days activity, which was great. I'm sure it was easier to deal with Libby in this environment than it normally is when we take them to the movies with the general public. The girls enjoy the films, of course (especially Libby), but they sometimes get a little excited and can make squealing noises or sit up and down in their seats a lot, which can lead to the inevitable tutting and huffing from other parents.

Back in February, to get the girls out and about one rainy morning during a school break, we took them to see the animated film Megamind. Both girls seemed to enjoy the film but, as is often the case, they did get over excited at times and make a bit of noise. This isn't too bad during noisy parts of the film, but is much more obvious during quieter moments, so you hope they keep their jabbering and squealing for the action sequences. Towards the end there was a very quiet and emotional scene, so I was hoping the girls would stay quiet and not ruin the moment for everyone else. Luckily, they didn't say a word and just watched the scene unfold. Then Liberty, very deliberately, leant forward in her seat and, as if it were the most acceptable thing in the world, let out the most enormous fart you can imagine. She then casually relaxed back into her seat, never once taking her eyes off the screen or showing even the slightest hint of feeling self conscious in any way. Karen and I rocked back and forth in our seats, simultaneously dying of both laughter and embarrassment.

I love the holidays, and I need a break from work as much as the next person, but you'll understand that there is always a small part of me that is a little relieved to get back to work after six weeks with the girls.

Robyn and Libby at the cinema. Be glad this isn't a scratch 'n' sniff picture

BLOG POST FROM JUNE 12 2011 - I THINK WE'RE ALONE NOW

Here we are in June, and outside we have a particularly strong example of a typical British summer's day. Yes, it's lashing down out there. A good week, then, for someone to decide to go off for a week to sunnier climes; and that's exactly what my lovely *wife Karen has done. 5 days ago, she boarded the Ryanair luxury jet to the Algarve in Portugal, leaving me to hold the fort with the three kids. I thought you might like to know how it's all going.*

Monday night I experienced solo Robyn-watch for the first time. As I will explain in more detail in another post, I had to get up to take her to the bathroom for toileting at 9pm, 10pm, 1am, 4am and then get her up to go again at 7am. This is what we do with Robyn every night, but it is something Karen and I share out, so we usually only have to get up once each in the dead of night. By myself this was going to be a different story, and I could tell when I got up for work on Tuesday that a week of this was going to take its toll.

Thankfully, Wednesday and Thursday night would see Robyn and Libby staying over at their residential hostel, so that would give me some crucial respite. So, I got up with the girls uniforms already ironed and ready to go. I have got them ready for school before, but it's not something I have to do very often; there's a reason that Karen is a stay-at-home mum. I got them dressed without any trouble and even successfully brushed their hair, though it's safe to say that the girls were going to be wearing alice band type things this week, rather than having their hair 'up', in plaits, pigtails, ponytails or any other stylish option; those are skills that Dad just doesn't have. I sorted out lunch for the three kids and moved onto breakfast: toast and hot chocolate for Liberty, bacon for Robyn and, as I had heard him say recently that he would like a heartier breakfast, bacon and eggs for George. I packed them all off to school and felt like Superdad.

I had informed Sam, my line manager at school and a good friend, about my situation for the week, so she knew that I might be slightly late on some days due to having to wait for the girls' taxi, but I got to school just a minute or two after registration started. In fact, Tuesday passed off without too much trouble at all, and on Wednesday morning I got the girls ready again and sent them off to school, noticing that Robyn had only picked at her bacon, but not thinking too much of it. I drove off for work with a relieved sigh. I would now have 56 girl-less hours, just looking after George and myself, before dealing with the weekend.

At 1.30pm, Sam came to me with a phone number to call one of the girls' schools; one of them was ill. I called the number and was told that Robyn had vomited on the way to school and again after lunch. I would have to go and pick her up. This meant getting permission to leave school early and drive the 80 minute journey from my school to Robyn's school. It meant that Robyn wouldn't be staying at residential that night or the night after, and I wouldn't be getting my two nights of uninterrupted sleep. It also meant that, because she had a sickness bug, I couldn't send her into school the next day. On the upside, I didn't have to teach my class of Year 9 boys, so every cloud...

My daughters rarely get ill, so what are the odds of one of the girls getting sick the exact week Karen is away? Well, as it happens, the odds are pretty damn good. In fact, had I have been walking past Ladbroke's bookmakers and noticed they were doing 'Karen Holiday Specials' and saw that one of the girls being sick while Karen was away was being offered at a 5-1 chance, I may well have been tempted to put a sneaky fiver on myself.

The only upside to the girls being ill is that they are very quiet and lethargic, which at least makes them easier to look after. Robyn spent the evening just lying on the settee with her iPad. This meant that George and I could take full advantage of the absence of his mother. I'm quite capable of cooking tasty, healthy meals, but where's the fun in that? We sent out for chicken fried rice and sweet & sour sauce from our local Chinese takeaway and the pair of us settled down for some father and son bonding time, stuffing ourselves whilst watching Man Vs Food. Awesome!

Robyn's school's strict quarantine rules mean that she can't go back to school for a couple of days following a bout of sickness, even though she seemed to be feeling fine the next morning. No school for Robyn meant that she was going to have to come with me to my school as, at such short notice, there really wasn't time to formulate a Plan B. I put her in her nicest Tinkerbell pyjamas so she would be comfortable, loaded a bag with Robyn friendly snacks, treats and her iPad and headphones (I do find it slightly depressing how often I refer to my favourite toy as 'Robyn's iPad'). At home we have a large 5' x 3' cushion, so I put that into the car, along with her quilt and pillow.

When we got to school I sent a bunch of kids from my form out to my car to collect all our stuff, and we built a little bed for Robyn in a corner of my classroom. If you have visions of an old fashioned English school with wooden floors, you are somewhat wide of the mark; our school has just been built and is carpeted and very modern. My room has 12 iMacs around the edge of the room on permanent display, so I'm sure Robyn felt reasonably at home.

It has to be said that Robyn was as good as we had any right to expect her to be. She happily watched films on the iPad and played games on the BBC CBeebies website on the computers. The kids thought she was unbelievably cute, and of course, she is. I also had to point out to some of them that she was actually older than they were. Every now and again she would get a little antsy, and I would take her out for a walk around the corridors. At lunch and break I took her for walks outside to get fresh air and to see the sheep and chickens that the school keeps for the students of the agricultural course. I also confiscated a football from some boys so Robyn and I could have a game of catch.

There was only one tricky moment, really. At one point, I needed to go to the toilet and, seeing Robyn lying engrossed in a film on the iPad, I left the class for a minute to dash down the corridor. The nearest toilet was locked, so I had to go to one slightly further away. As I hurried back, I turned onto the English corridor and bumped into Robyn who had seized her moment to escape. Seriously, what was I thinking? As the Shakespearean saying goes, all's well that ends well, but had I been delayed by just another 30 seconds, I can imagine all manner of disastrous consequences as Robyn was let loose on an unsuspecting high school. Still, it could have been worse, and had it have been Liberty who was ill, it certainly would have been. In fact, had Libby been ill, I don't think I would have entertained the idea of taking her to work with me at all. Important GCSEs or not, the kids would have had to do without me for a day.

Friday was a staff training day where I was supposed to be creating working documents for the Media department. Robyn not going to school meant I had permission to work from home, so her illness wasn't all bad! It should also be said that once Robyn came home on Wednesday she wasn't sick once, nor did she show any sign of actually feeling ill, which is about par for the course, so I wasn't exactly running around cleaning up after a kid who had turned into a vomit fountain.

Saturday afternoon was my personal highlight of the week. George was out with friends, the girls were out with careworkers and, after I had taken care of the laundry and the shopping, I had about an hour on my own at home, watching my favourite show of the moment ('The Good Wife'), eating Swiss chocolate and drinking Mountain Dew. The only sound I could hear was the television; pressing pause on the TV meant I could just hear the birds outside. Bliss. Absolute bliss.

I don't find looking after the girls and George too difficult. The tricky part of this week has been dealing with everything domestically, including getting Robyn up in the night, and working full time as well. I know there are plenty of parents who do something similar every day, so I don't give myself too much credit for doing what needed to be done. Karen needed a break, and she *would do the same for me. Being quite domesticated I can cook, clean and wash without any real concerns, but I do struggle with the traditional male responsibilities in the house; Karen usually takes care of those. When I changed a battery in a smoke alarm yesterday, I was so impressed with myself I half expected to hear a round of applause.*

❦

PRESENT DAY

Liberty's lack of understanding of social conventions can lead to some difficult situations. A few years back, she developed a big love of the film 'Who Framed Roger Rabbit?' and particularly for the character of the voluptuous Jessica Rabbit. Libby loved to slink about the house in a sultry manner, suggestively singing 'Why Don't You Do Right' like Jessica Rabbit does in a smoky club in the movie. For Libby, she was just singing a song and doing a bit of a dance like she saw in her favourite film, with no understanding of the sexual connotations of her performance. Of course, it's slightly disconcerting for a father to watch his sixteen year-old additional needs daughter performing in such a way, and it doesn't help that Libby is such an effective mimic, perfectly copying Jessica's breathy vocals.

We then found out that Liberty wanted to take her copying of Jessica Rabbit to the next level when going through her iPad videos that she makes of herself. Libby loves to film herself acting out scenes from films which she likes to watch and rewatch, and they can be very entertaining for others, too. It can also be incriminating for Libby as we have found clips she has made of herself doing things like starting fires in the house, and making handprints on the windows all around the house with a bowl of icing. When you find these videos, usually when going through the clips to delete some of them as her iPad is full, you can show them to Libby and tell her off and tell her that 'starting fires is very naughty'. Her usual response is to repeatedly say that she's sorry, but you suspect that she is saying this because she has learned that this is what she is supposed to say in such circumstances, rather than because she feels any sort of actual contrition, and she then says it repeatedly because she rather likes the way it sounds.

One of the videos I found when deleting her filmed clips was one of her doing a full performance of 'Why Don't You Do Right?' in full Jessica Rabbit mode. And while we had seen her do this on many occasions, this performance added something a little extra in terms of her outfit. Obviously feeling that her typical jeans and t-shirt weren't especially conducive to channelling the sexy Jessica Rabbit, Libby had gone in to her Mum's wardrobe and borrowed her red high heels and a red silky garment that, shall we say, is usually reserved for more private occasions.

This led to Liberty asking for a Jessica Rabbit outfit for her birthday. Libby could see from her calendar that her birthday was just a week or two before Halloween, and we always attend a fancy dress party on this occasion, so she wanted an outfit of a sequinned strapless dress, long red wig and elbow length silky gloves, that could be worn for her videos and also for the fancy dress parade. I wasn't a fan of the idea. I only mention this next piece of information because it has relevance to the story, but Libby has a curvy figure and the idea of her filling out a Jessica Rabbit outfit didn't make this Dad thrilled. However, as is often the case, Dads get overruled, though I was somewhat mollified by the promise that she would wear a skin-coloured upper body-suit beneath her strapless dress.

When Libby unwrapped the dress and put it on, it was very clear that the bodysuit would be needed, though it was also clear that she didn't want to wear it. In fairness to Libby, I understood that; after all, Jessica Rabbit didn't wear anything underneath her strapless dress and, around the house, that wasn't so much of a problem as long as we didn't have guests. My Mum and Dad came over on the evening of her birthday to see her blow out the candles with Libby wearing her new strapless dress; my poor Dad didn't know where he was supposed to look. I wanted to put a photo of her wearing the full outfit on her Facebook page, but the only photo that I could get of her wearing the dress without the bodysuit that was remotely appropriate for public consumption was from behind. The bodysuit provided a pleasing amount of cover and made the outfit feel much less revealing, even if it wasn't quite what your grandmother might call 'modest'.

When Halloween came around, Libby was not for wearing the bodysuit beneath the dress. I didn't want to be the kind of Dad who says, 'You're not going out dressed like that', but, trust me, if you saw her in that Jessica Rabbit outfit, you'd have insisted on the bodysuit, too. And here was the clincher, the fancy dress party she was going to was being held at church.

The bodysuit was not negotiable. However, Libby seemed to think it was, and point blank refused to wear it. She seemed to think that if she screamed and shouted enough then we would back down and change our minds, but neither Karen or I were about to walk Libby into a church building for a children's party with her in her full Jessica Rabbit outfit. Every time I thought about changing my mind, I imagined everyone's reaction as I walked into the church hall with our 16 year-old autistic daughter dressed as some sort of strumpet. We reached an impasse. Libby went absolutely postal in her bid to get her way and refused to put the bodysuit on; we wouldn't take her until she did.

One of the few angles of Libby's Jessica Rabbit dress that was acceptable to her Dad

In the end, Karen got Robyn (dressed as an enchanted

Cinderella, as always) and put her in the car and drove away. Only when Libby saw that we were actually willing to go without her did she finally relent. It was high stakes poker, but the parents won out, this time. Libby put the bodysuit on, Karen came back to get us, and she went along to the party and had a perfectly lovely time.

Libby at the fancy dress party in Jessica Rabbit dress with, you'll notice, bodysuit underneath. Robyn as Cinderella is in the background

❧ 8 ❧

YOU NEED TO CALM DOWN - SLEEP AND NIGHTTIME

BLOG POST FROM JANUARY 23 2011 - DON'T BE CRUEL (TO A HEART THAT'S TRUE)

I t's early Saturday morning. Due to work on weekdays and commitments I have at church on a Sunday, I can only attempt a lie in on a Saturday morning. And yet, here I am, up at stupid o'clock, long before daylight, watching the news and writing this. Any parent of an autistic child won't be particularly surprised at this turn of events, as it is one of the cruellest elements of looking after our kids.

For the uninitiated, let me explain. Autism brings with it all kinds of unusual behaviour. There's the social awkwardness, the pedantic eating habits, the seeming allergy to clothes, the escaping from your house on a regular basis so you have to call the police, the pooing on the front window sill in full view of the street, the smearing of said poo up the walls of your lounge and, as they used to say on those ads for compilation albums, many, many more!

This makes life, shall we say, challenging. But here's the thing. I have a couple of horrible weeks coming up at work that I am approaching with dread (how lucky I am to be an educator). However, I know that, come February 5th, I will be filled with an enormous sense of well being. This tough little fortnight will be *over and I will be able to look forward to work being a little more relaxed. But our family life is rather different.*

When Robyn and Liberty are at their stunning best, when they've broken my 32Gb iPod Touch for the 17th time, when they've thrashed the house to within an inch of its life for the third time that day, when we've bid farewell to the police after they've found 12 year old Robyn knee deep in cow crap at a local farm, or she's decided yet again that wearing nappies isn't for her and then lies in bed and pees like a racehorse making the house stink of urine, I know that this isn't going to be over in a fortnight. This isn't going to be over next year. In fact, I can look forward to this kind of thing maybe every day of my life, probably till the day I die.

So when both girls decide that 3 or 4 or 5 am is a good time to get up on a Saturday morning, shouting loudly, getting in our bed and talking to themselves loudly, setting the treadmill going (loudly) in the room directly beneath our bedroom, playing Toy Story 3 on the iPad at full volume and deciding that the ultimate venue for this viewing experience is under your covers where you're trying to sleep, well, I can't help thinking it's the cruellest blow of all.

My daughters are beautiful and funny and you should never doubt that I love them with all my heart. But sometimes you can't help thinking, after all of the trials and traumas that autism drags kicking and screaming into the house, is it really asking too much to have a lie in on a Saturday morning?

PRESENT DAY

Another very early blog, that one. In fact, it was the second one I wrote. You can tell this by the way it's short (up to 500 words this time), and I'm still just making some observations, rather than building those observations around stories. But the style is there.

BLOG POST FROM APRIL 8 2011 - OOPS!... I DID IT AGAIN

Many of us would say that our children are our number one priority in life. Some might say they are our entire world, maybe even our reason to exist. So what does it say about us that we completely treasure the time we have away from them? What is better than a day, or even a weekend, without the kids? For me, nothing; but I always find that it's lovely to be back with them when we come home again.

On Wednesday and Thursday nights, Robyn and Liberty stay over at a residential home for kids with autism. There they do all kinds of stimulating activities and have a wonderful time. There is always a spring in their step on a Wednesday morning when they head off to their taxi with their suitcases. However, like us, they like to come home again. They are at their most relaxed when they are here. So, I don't feel so bad about enjoying a bit of time away from the girls; they enjoy a bit of time away from me, too.

Of course, the thing I enjoy the most about the girls being away is the uninterrupted sleep. The girls are quite good about going to bed these days, but they've not always been so cooperative when it's come to staying there. In 2008, the council built an extension to our house to allow the girls to have separate bedrooms (I've never said there weren't upsides to our family circumstances).

We had a three bedroom house with a son and two daughters. In that situation, there isn't much of an alternative to the two girls sharing a bedroom. Unfortunately, this meant that the girls got very little sleep as one of them would always keep the other awake with their constant squealing and jabbering, which would in turn keep everyone else in the house awake. We had to take the light bulb permanently out of their room because they wouldn't entertain the idea of sleep if they had access to light. Now they have their own rooms and they do have light bulbs, but the light switches are outside of their bedroom and the doors can be locked if necessary. In truth, they rarely need to be locked in at night these days as they have got used to being in the dark.

The girls sleeping in separate rooms has greatly increased the amount of sleep we all get, but there are still issues. Both girls are toilet trained during the day without any problems at all, but both need to wear nappies (diapers) at night, though this isn't really a problem in itself. That is until Robyn decided that she was now too grown up to wear nappies, but not sufficiently grown up to take herself to the toilet in the night. This meant that she would wet the bed every single night. After a while her bed had to be thrown away, but Robyn had already decided she preferred sleeping on the floor anyway. Soon, she ended up with no carpet (which had also been destroyed by urine) and no bed, just a thin plastic mattress and her ever present quilt, which had to be washed every night. I am not exaggerating when I tell you that there were times when I would put her to 'bed', watching her scuttle away to lie on the floorboards, and I would feel like some evil guardian from a Dickens novel.

After a while, we put a decent quality cushioned linoleum flooring down which made me feel a bit better, but she still ended up sleeping on the floor, wrapped in her quilt, most nights. We knew from her nights sleeping away at residential that she preferred sleeping on the floor even when she had a bed and, with her refusal to wear a nappy at night, a carpet was out of the question. But recently we decided to give Robyn and a bed another go. We knew it may well turn out to be an enormous waste of money as she may not even sleep in the thing, and we also knew that buying a cheap one wasn't really an option either;

she wasn't likely to opt to sleep in a bed if it wasn't even that comfortable. Thankfully, she has decided that she rather likes her new bed and is happy to sleep in it. I can't tell you what it's done for my parental self respect to be able to tuck my daughter into a proper bed, rather than watch her rolling up in a quilt on bare floorboards.

There was still one big issue left. Urine. Going into Robyn's room to wake her up without a breathing mask could turn out to be a mistake that was hazardous to your health. Every morning her room used to smell like an old people's home where the cleaners were on strike. Forgive me for this detail (particularly if you're eating any time soon) but it was always the worst the night after she'd had 3 or 4 bowls of bolognese. I'm not going to lie to you, it was Gag City in there, believe me. Clearly, a new bed was not going to last long if that bathroom behaviour continued, so there had to be a plan.

We knew she got through the night 'dry' at residential, so we found out how they did it. It was quite simple; at various intervals in the night, a carer would get her out of bed and take her to the bathroom. The thing is, at the residential centre there is obviously someone whose job it is to stay up all night to ensure there are no problems with the children; they can easily undertake the task

of getting Robyn up to go to the bathroom every few hours. Funnily enough, we don't have someone like that who lives at our house, so it's all down to us. I used to go to bed and set my alarm clock for the morning like anyone else. Now my night goes like this:

9pm – take Robyn to the bathroom (make sure she actually goes for a wee – it's not unknown for the little minx to only pretend to go and then wet the bed straight away) and then put her to bed.

Immediately go to bed myself. Robyn's like Bagpuss – when she goes to sleep, all her friends go to sleep.

Read for a while, but when I can feel I'm about to go to sleep (usually around 10pm) go and get Robyn back up to take her to the bathroom.

Back to bed and set my alarm for midnight.

Midnight – get up and take Robyn to the bathroom.

3am – Karen gets up to take Robyn to the bathroom.

6am – Get up and take Robyn to the bathroom, then I get ready for work.

7am – Karen gets Robyn up to get ready for school, obviously making sure she goes to the bathroom first.

Believe it or not, even with all that, we still don't always get a dry night. But my little girl does get to sleep in a bed. And when all is said and done, I've decided that her comfort, and my need not to feel like Fagin, is more important than me getting a full night's sleep. Or the smell of urine.

Robyn and Dad getting used to her new bed

✤ 9 ✤

NEVER GROW UP - PHILOSOPHY
ON AUTISM
PRESENT DAY

T his blog was posted just before Robyn became a teenager. It was certainly an occasion for reflecting on how different her life was, and how different our family life was as a result of their autism. Such reflection often brings out the best in my writing, and I think this was one of my favourite blog posts.

BLOG POST FROM FEBRUARY 26 2011 - TEENAGE DREAM

Robyn turns 13 this weekend. My little girl is now a teenager; a situation that only serves to highlight the differences between Robyn and her peers. And although I'm thinking about Robyn today, most of what I'm writing applies equally to Liberty.

When the girls were quite young, a family friend asked me whether I had 'mourned' yet for our loss; that is, to come to terms with the things we would never get to do with our daughters. Until that time I hadn't really looked that far into the future. I suppose I was too busy cleaning poo off the walls to think much farther than getting to bed that night. But it can be quite sobering when you start to think about how different your family life will be, and you then begin to think about the expectations you had for your kids, without ever really realising it.

I don't imagine that many people bring children into the world thinking about landmark days and relationships that their children will have. I'm sure that, for most people, having kids is something of an instinctive need, rather than a thought out plan. But when your children have serious special needs of one kind or another, it forces you to face up to the harsh reality of the future that will never be, and how much you had unwittingly invested in it.

There are many important events we have already missed, and as I look forward to the future, I realise there are plenty more events and experiences that will never be. We won't ever get up on an August morning to take the girls to school to get their GCSE and A-Level results, and that would have been something special. Robyn and Liberty are clearly such bright girls, but their under-standing of the world around them is so very limited that they can't even begin to access the traditional school curriculum. I'd have loved to see Robyn graduate from university. I think she, in particu-lar, would have been academically successful, and in my mind's eye I can see her in her gown and mortarboard, looking fabulous.

Robyn won't go through other rites of passage that teenagers go through either, such as going to her high school Prom. Quite why I feel sad that I won't have to spend the thick end of a grand on a dress, shoes, hair and nails just for her to attend a glorified disco, I don't know. But I do.

At church, our children are baptised when they are 8 years old. At that age it is felt that children are accountable for what they know and able to choose right from wrong. As this is the criterion, Robyn will never need to be baptised as she can never *technically know right from wrong; anyone who's seen her laughing to herself when she's been caught sneaking the last of the Pepsi from the fridge will doubt whether or not this is actually true, but that's the official situation. So, from a doctrinal viewpoint, this shouldn't make any difference to us – but it's another rite of passage in which we won't participate. Another special family occasion that will go uncelebrated.*

And, of course, I will never get to walk either of my little girls down the aisle at their wedding. They are light years from being able to form those kinds of relationships. And I think, when I imagine what that day might have been like, that one more than any other breaks my heart.

However, I wouldn't want you to think that the glass is entirely half empty. As I often like to say, when people change their circumstances in life, they generally trade one set of problems for a new set of problems. But the reverse is also true. We've had to trade many of the traditional experiences parents have with their children for different ones, and this isn't totally a bad thing. Consider this:

Robyn doesn't want to watch trashy, sweary TV – she still loves to watch her Disney movies. Robyn doesn't want to wear short skirts and low-cut tops – she's happy to wear the pretty clothes her mum buys for her. Robyn never complains about how embarrassing her parents are or refuses to be seen with us in public – she's quite happy to be the one who embarrasses everyone else. Robyn doesn't want to go out with friends of whom we don't approve till all hours – she doesn't have any friends. Robyn doesn't spend every waking second on her Blackberry or iPhone – she's great with technology but doesn't have the understanding of language to text or make calls. Robyn never makes sassy remarks or answers back – she doesn't talk at all. And Robyn hasn't got an older boyfriend making inappropriate amorous advances for which I would feel duty bound to purchase a shotgun – she has no comprehension of how to even begin a romance.

So, on this auspicious day in Robyn's life, I'm reminded of an old truism. Swings and roundabouts, people, swings and round-abouts. I love my little girl, and I'm so blessed she is a part of my life. Most other dads may get to take their daughter to the Prom, see them graduate and walk them down the aisle. But my little girl will stay my little girl forever more, no matter how many years go by.

PRESENT DAY

And she still is. In fact, because of the way our relationships with the girls developed, Robyn and I are closer than ever. She rarely responds to people who visit these days. She used to give out high fives and fist bumps but, for whatever reason, she is reluc-tant to do so now. But Dad always gets big hugs and snuggles whenever she sees me. When Robyn is home for the weekend, I let her get on with her iPad or watching a movie or whatever it is she's doing, but I'll go over every so often to grab a cuddle. Because Robyn doesn't talk, a hug is the best way to interact with her, and then get right up in her face and talk in an animated fashion. And, when I do, the technology gets put aside and she looks me in the eyes and smiles. Robyn will always love Disney, but Daddy is still her favourite.

Robyn did, in fact, get to go to a Prom at her high school and her college. Of course, Robyn wouldn't have understood anything about why she'd got a new dress and why someone was doing her nails for her, but she likes dressing up and likes disco lights and music, so I'm sure she enjoyed it. It certainly wouldn't have been the same as the Prom that the kids at the high school where I taught went to, but we appreciate that the staff at her school went to the trouble. I suspect, to some extent, they actually do these things as much for the parents of their students than the students themselves, so we can feel like we have been included in the rites of passage that other kids get to have.

The next blog was a bit of a controversial one. I addressed the issue of therapy and medication for autistic kids. I'll reiterate what I said in the blog post, because my opinion hasn't really changed. We didn't feel that intensive therapies like ABA (applied behavioural analysis) were appropriate for our girls. As I explain in the blog post, we looked into them and just didn't feel Robyn or Libby would respond well to that type of therapy. But that doesn't mean it doesn't work for others. A relative of ours also has autism and went through ABA therapy which helped him enormously. So, there's no judgement here, but I explain why we felt that we were happy to just let our girls live their lives as they were.

BLOG POST FROM MARCH 25 2011 - LIVE YOUR LIFE BE FREE

'It's a dog's life', people say, and it's a saying that I've never understood. It's a phrase that's usually said to imply that a dog's life is not an enviable one when, from what I can see, a dog's life is pretty damn good. As long as you've got a decent owner, you get provided with meals, get taken out for some fun and exercise a couple of times a day, and the rest of the time you get to lounge around, hogging all the heat from the fire while people tickle your tummy. Seriously, what's not to like? Does a dog have to worry about paying the mortgage or cope with complex adult relationships? Does a dog have to teach English to a class of naughty 14 year-olds at the end of a Wednesday afternoon? No, it jolly well does not.

What has this got to do with my family? It's quite simple. I believe that Robyn and Liberty, despite their condition, have a pretty great life. They go to school and really enjoy the stimulating activities they do there, and how many other kids can truly say the same? They come home and get to eat their favourite foods all the time ('Don't even try to give me anything new that I won't like – I'm autistic, remember?'). After that they can watch their films, look at websites and play with toys and games. Other than very occasionally tidying up after themselves, they never have to do any chores or homework and they basically get waited on hand and foot.

Some people, including some parents of autistic children, would disagree with my assessment of the situation. They feel that kids with autism are not really experiencing life by living in their own rather limited world. It's a fair point. Some autistic kids are very aware of how different they are, but Libby & Robyn genuinely seem completely oblivious. They really do seem happy with the life they live.

The thing is, there is no cure for autism. There are treatments that can make a difference with some children, but Karen and I have never been in favour of putting our kids through intensive therapy. That's not to say that those who choose to go down that avenue are wrong; just that it isn't what we want for our daughters. For me, and this is just my point of view, it comes down to questions like these: Is the way that 'normal' people live their lives the only way to live? If someone can't function and interact in the ways that are typical in our society, is their existence just a waste of time? Do we really want to traumatise our children with difficult treatment just because they're not living their lives the way other children do?

Let me tell you a story. It was December 25th 2000. Christmas morning. George was four years old, Robyn was nearly three (not yet diagnosed) and Liberty had just been born. This would be the last Christmas morning that we would spend at my in-laws. After this, we were a sufficiently established family unit to celebrate Christmas by ourselves. But this was a Christmas morning that is indelibly etched on our memories for other reasons. Not because it brought us the fun and excitement that one normally associates with Christmas, but because it saw the shadow of autism loom ever larger over our lives.

In Karen's family they have a tradition that everyone watches everyone else open their presents on Christmas morning, starting with the youngest. Starting with Robyn. Robyn has never been overly interested in wrapped presents; I don't think she can see the point. Her attitude seems to say, 'If you've got a nice toy to give me, just hand it over – why are you making it difficult for me?' Imagine for a minute that you don't understand the concept of what a surprise is, and you can see her point.

So, we helped her unwrap a present that we knew she would like: a set of Teletubby dolls. Once she'd got them out of their plastic packaging she was thrilled, and started to play with them straight away. In fact, she was so engrossed that we couldn't get her remotely interested in any of her other presents. With George waiting anxiously to open his gifts, we decided to move on.

The in-laws tradition of everyone opening presents individually means that it's a rather drawn out affair. Still, Robyn spent the entire time lining up her Teletubbies in order; Tinky-winky, Dipsy, La-La, then Po. She'd put them up in a line and take them back down. Put them up, take them down. When everyone had finished opening their presents it was over an hour later, and yet Robyn was still lining up and taking down her Teletubbies. As Karen watched her, she suddenly burst into tears at the realisation of how different our life was going to be with Robyn. This was not how she imagined Christmas morning with her young family. Karen is more than willing to acknowledge that having a breakdown on Christmas morning is a bit of a downer for everyone else who just want to open presents and tuck into a breakfast of Quality Street chocolates, but that's how these things pan out sometimes.

Robyn playing with her Teletubbies on Christmas
morning in 2000

As I held Karen in my arms, trying to soothe and console her, I did something unusual for me; I said something quite wise. I turned Karen to look at a smiling Robyn, engrossed in her *play. 'Look', I said, 'she's happy. That's all that really matters'. It was a big turning point in us being able to accept Robyn for who she was, rather than what we had originally expected her to be.*

When people are surprised at the positivity that Karen and I have about our situation, they should realise that it all comes back to this: we are perfectly happy for our girls to be autistic. It may not have been the family life we would have chosen, but you only need to spend a short amount of time with Robyn and Liberty to know that they are entirely content with their place in the world. Others would implement therapy to try and make them a little more like us, and they're entitled to make that choice for their children. But we're not willing to risk Robyn and Libby's happiness by dragging them kicking and screaming into a world they don't understand.

BLOG POST FROM APRIL 16 2011 - HOLD ME, THRILL ME, KISS ME, KILL ME

Sky Atlantic recently showed the film Temple Grandin starring Clare Danes as the famous pioneering engineer and awareness raiser for autism. As a parent of two autistic kids, you do rather feel duty bound to watch something when there's a strong autistic angle, and I'm glad I did; it was excellent. There was a touching scene towards the end where Temple hugs her mother for the first time, which really made me think. A classic symptom for some people with autism, across the spectrum, is shunning physical contact. Some autistic children and adults just cannot bare to be held, hugged or even touched. As you may know by now, Liberty and Robyn's autism is at the upper end of the spectrum. Therefore, we have always been grateful that our daughters are extremely affectionate and tactile. For me, it is one benefit that makes many other problems that autism brings more bearable.

Liberty does have issues with touching, but not the ones you might expect. If anything, she is too affectionate. With those she is familiar with, particularly her mum and dad, she thinks nothing of jumping on your lap and burying her face into your neck to smother you with kisses. Cute? Sure. Though not always as cute as you might think when I'm trying to watch the Spurs game on television. It isn't always just mum and dad, though. Libby's affection can be bestowed upon anybody she likes the look of. People have visited our house for the first time and been rather taken aback by this Disney quoting child who insists on slobbering on their necks. I've noticed she's more likely to grant her favours to attractive people though; male or female, she's not really bothered! They don't even need to be in our house. Her carers brought her back last Saturday and told us, ('just to let you know') she had been snuggling up to the girl next to her on the swing in the park.

Robyn is not as generous with her favours as Libby, but she does not object to being touched. She will come over and sit on your knee and snuggle up to you but, as with almost everything with Robyn, there is usually an ulterior motive that is beneficial only to her. When she comes and sits with me I know that it won't be very long at all before she takes my hands and puts them on her ribs; Robyn loves to be tickled. Also beware when Robyn comes and grants you a kiss. People are always flattered and thrilled when Robyn plants a smacker on their lips, but we always have a slightly more cynical look on our faces. If Robyn gives you a kiss, she wants something. The kiss will almost always be accompanied by her taking your hand and dragging you somewhere to get her something, often something she's not supposed to have.

Robyn also has some very particular fetishes. She likes to sit on people's knees and touch their necks while they talk. One assumes it's a sensory thing and she likes the vibrations. Something else she does, which is slightly awkward in these racially sensitive times, is gravitate towards black people. Our ethnic group is plain old White British, and we don't live in the most ethnically varied area, so people with darker skin are slightly unusual visitors to our house. When Robyn plants herself on the knee of friends from Ghana and Trinidad and starts stroking their face whilst smiling at them, we have to say a little apologetically, 'She likes black people'. So far, no-one has been offended.

Liberty has some less friendly touching habits. As she speaks in echolalia, one of the phrases you will hear her say is, 'No pinching!', which tells you she must hear from her parents all the time. When Libby is frustrated she grabs your arm and shouts. With me, that's all she does. I tell her not to pinch and she lets go, probably because I can sound quite scary when I need to. She treats my wife differently though, and Karen's forearms are often covered in bruises where Libby has gone for those little pinches that cause maximum pain and lasting marks. Unfortunately, we are not the only recipients of Liberty's 'violence' and we often get reports home from school and church that she has 'attacked' someone. This makes you feel bad, but at the same time you know there isn't really much you can do about it. It isn't a question of upbringing or discipline; it's a question of Libby's autism and her being unable to process her own frustration.

Robyn also reacts when she gets frustrated, but she makes herself the victim of her own aggression. She bites her own arms when she isn't being understood or can't get what she wants, and her forearms are often scarred and chapped where she has self-harmed. It's always an upsetting sight to see her this distressed and we always rush over to stop her. But, as I'm writing, I'm wondering if, given the choice, I would prefer the girls to inflict harm on themselves or others. And I genuinely don't know what my honest answer is.

To end on a more positive note, Robyn always seems to know when it's time for Saturday Morning Snuggles. On other mornings she will get up and go downstairs to start getting ready to go out, but on Saturdays she seems to know that no-one has to hurry anywhere. She climbs into our bed in her pyjamas and snuggles up to me and, for the only time in the week, she doesn't seem to have any ulterior motive. We often fire up the iPad and I check Facebook and my emails and she puts her head on my shoulder and her arm across my chest and stares intently at what I'm reading. She did it this morning, though it didn't create such a warm and fuzzy today; principally because she'd been downstairs eating Cheesy Wotsits and was then breathing in my face.

But I know that many parents of children with autism would love to share such moments with their kids, so it would be deeply ungracious of me not to acknowledge just how lucky we are in this respect. There may be so many issues with my girls that cause us stress, difficulty and heartache, but the kisses, hugs and snuggles I get from my girls are one of the greatest blessings in my life.

Robyn in tactile mood. She was obviously in a good mood as the necklace I'm wearing was one she made for me

PRESENT DAY

The girls are still tactile and affectionate, but now they are both in their twenties so it's very much on their own terms. Liberty is always very affectionate with her mother, and some other family and friends, almost always female. As I addressed elsewhere, poor old Dad over here has been very much left aside in Libby's affections. Because I do so much for her, Karen will nag Libby to 'give Daddy a kiss' to say thank you. In very recent times, she has been a little more liberal with her affectionate favours, and that's been very rewarding.

Robyn still loves snuggle time with Dad. I know she's 23, and that may seem weird to some, but they're just going to have to get over it. Robyn isn't a typical 23 year-old; not by a long shot. When she comes home for the weekend, she still jumps in Mum and Dad's bed at bedtime to cuddle up to us and look at my phone with me as I'm scrolling. If you're going to talk to Robyn, given that she shows very little in terms of response to what you say, there's not much point in casually talking to her from across the room. You need to get right in her face, eye to eye, and talk in a very engaging manner. That's how you communicate with Robyn. She may not understand much in the way of individual words, but she'll pick up on your tone and expression. Her main response when I do that is laughter, and that's always lovely.

It's a strange thing to look back on, just how much more interaction we had with Robyn at the age of 13 than we do now she's 23. There are parts in the blog post where I talk about her putting my hands on her ribs to tickle her, or bringing a fork to us to let us know she was hungry; she just doesn't do that anymore. She would do other things, too, that seem amazing when I look back. She used to choose which film she wanted to watch and communicate that to us. Before the era of tablets and smartphones, we had moved away from DVDs because the girls were just breaking them and it was annoying and stupidly expensive. Instead, we had the Disney Movie Channel and we'd record the films on our personal video recorder. Then I laminated a small photo of each film we had on our PVR and put them on a keyring. Robyn could then flick through the pictures until she got to the film she wanted and give it to me; then I could put that film on for her.

Robyn does not deliberately communicate with us in any of those ways anymore. And it's not just that Robyn doesn't communicate; she doesn't do anything at home for herself, other than eat her own food and use her own iPad or laptop. It isn't that Robyn's mental skills or physical abilities have regressed; I don't doubt that Robyn could still do all of those things if she wanted to but, for some reason, she doesn't want to do that at this time. I think they have a little more success with her at her residence, but then they're paid to be one on one with her and have all that time to be patient with her.

Robyn's latest thing, as a for instance, when we're going down the stairs, is just to stand at the top of the stairs. She won't come down until I go back to the top of the stairs and grab her hand, and then she'll come downstairs with me. She's been able to go to the toilet by herself for years but, when she's home now, she won't go unless you actually take her to the bathroom and tell her to sit down. I think some of this is a reaction to her moving out, but there's no real way of knowing why she chooses to act this way, and we don't know if or when it will change.

You might be forgiven for thinking that if you left Robyn for long enough, then necessity would lead to her taking the responsibility for herself, and she would ask for things or do more things for herself. You'd think that, but it really isn't so. At the moment, we have to remember to take her to the toilet every few hours. There have been one or two occasions where we've forgotten for most of the day, because it is not usual to have to remember to take an adult to the bathroom when they've previously been quite capable of taking themselves. You feel really guilty about that when you suddenly remember, and then you take her to the toilet and she pees like a cow standing on a flat rock. You'd think, if you'd taken yourself to the loo many times before in your life, and you're completely confident about where it is and what to do, and you were desperate to go, then you'd just go, right? Nope. And there's a much worse story to tell about how determined Robyn is to do what she wants, or rather, not do what she doesn't want to do.

There were a couple of years where all the family went to church except Libby, whose behaviour had become so problematic that it just wasn't worth the risk anymore. There were quite a few incidents that led to this decision being taken, but the one that sticks in my mind was when, in the middle of the main church service, Libby went up to the microphone and started singing a song from the recently released Disney smash, High School Musical. From Libby's perspective, she can just see a microphone, and she knows from previous experience when she's been at church during the week without anyone around, that if you speak on the live microphone then your voice is amplified through the speakers in a way that all small kids find really fun. She's also seen people on TV use microphones when they're singing, so she gets to act out being a real singer. Why wouldn't she want to jump on the mic and drop some of her own dope vocal stylings? What do you mean we're in the middle of the main church service and we're all supposed to be reverent and quiet? How exactly am I ruining the church experience for everyone?

Well, initially, it might have been cute and a bit funny for the congregation to have Libby get up and sing in the middle of the main Sunday service, if not exactly appropriate. But, of course, we had to dash up to the pulpit to pull her away and explain that this wasn't the time for her to start singing 'Breaking Free'. And then it kicked off in a way that wasn't remotely cute or funny. Libby refused to budge from the pulpit, and we ended up having to physically remove her from the building. With my Mum and Karen, we picked her up the best that we could, but she was kicking and screaming with a violence that foreshadowed her behaviour in her later teenage years. I can still remember the silence in the chapel other than Libby's screams, and feeling every eye on us as we did our best to carry her out. I'm not sure how the meeting recovered after that, because we certainly didn't get to return.

So, with Liberty unable to attend church, Karen or I would usually stay at home with her, but we also had a rota of family and close friends who were willing to take the risk of a few hours in the house with her. The four of us arrived home from church one Sunday when my brother and his wife had been on what we called 'Libby Watch'. I don't recall all the details but, right as we pulled up outside the house, there was something of a commotion. I seem to remember it was something to do with a wasp sting, but I could be wrong. We all dashed into the house to help out with the situation. The problem was quickly resolved and my brother and his wife left.

We were due to go out to one of our parents for lunch that day, but we had a sit down for a while first. After about 45 minutes, we started to think about getting ready to go. As was often the case, Karen went to get Libby ready, and I went to get Robyn. I went up to her room to get her, as she had a habit at the time of coming in and going straight to her room to lie down for a while whenever we'd been out. However, she wasn't there. As I looked around the house and called out to her I couldn't find her anywhere. It was a warm, summery day, so I checked if she'd gone out to the garden, to lie on the trampoline or play on the swing, but she wasn't there, either. Then I had an awful thought. I went out to the car, parked in the street, and there she was, just sitting there.

You see, Robyn sometimes goes through phases where she won't open the car door. Like the princess she is, she sits and waits for someone to come and open it for her, and then she'll happily jump out. As I said, this goes in phases, because there are other times when she willingly opens the door and gets out by herself, so it's certainly not about understanding or ability to operate the door handle. But this was during a time when she wasn't opening the door. The commotion as we had arrived meant that we had all dashed in and not made sure that Robyn had got out of the car. So she had just sat there. In a hot car without any windows open. For 45 minutes. She had the ability to get out at any time. She was perfectly capable of operating the door handle. She just wouldn't.

As you would expect, she was very hot, sweaty, dehydrated and seemed quite out of it. We got her into the house, got her to drink lots of water, stripped her down and got her into a cool shower to get her body temperature down. She was quickly back to normal, and there was no long term harm done, but it was a huge 'What if?' situation. What if we hadn't have been going out? We'd have probably assumed she was happily lying down in her room and just left her to it; let sleeping dogs lie, as we always say when the girls aren't causing any trouble. She could have been in that car for another hour before we'd thought to check her room to see if she was OK and found she wasn't there.

And so, the big question, the awful question, is would Robyn rather have died than open that car door? Was her compulsion to follow her behaviours and not get out of a hot car so great that she would have sat there, overheating, sweating, deeply uncomfortable, until she collapsed from heat exhaustion and expired? It seems incredible, but I honestly think that her state of mind is such that she literally *couldn't* open that door, regardless of the consequences. When we use hyperbole when talking about something we don't want to do and we say 'I'd rather die than...', of course, we don't actually mean it. But I think we've seen enough from Robyn to know that if she refuses to do something, she'd actually rather die than go against her own compulsions. As a father, that's a pretty damn sobering thought.

At the moment she is doing very little for herself while at home. Honestly, her commitment to not doing anything is quite remarkable. Not content with me opening the car door for her and ushering her to her seat, she will actually sit there with one leg in the car and the other outside the car, waiting for me to actually move her leg into the car for her. Getting her out of bed in the morning won't happen until you have actually gone into her room and taken her hand first. Even getting undressed, which she is altogether capable of doing, requires additional prompts. Taking her to the shower recently, she stood there, pyjama bottoms and underwear around her ankles, stubbornly refusing to just step out of them, until her legs are more or less moved for her so she can then get in the shower.

In the final blog in this chapter, I wanted to convey my philosophy on fatherhood and masculinity. Occasionally, back when I wrote the blog, I would get my thoughts down, read it back and think: nailed it. It's not always easy to access the random thoughts in your head and get them down on paper in a coherent and readable way. But the section towards the end where I discuss 'what does it mean to be a man'? That is really how I feel. Not just how I feel about my daughters, but how I feel about life and the role of men in modern society. I've never been especially macho or what society deemed as masculine. I've never been in a fight in my life. And I can't help but think that, in these times where people so readily talk of the patriarchy and toxic masculinity, the world might be a better a place if more of us subscribed to a gentler definition of masculinity.

And one other thing. There's a section where I discuss the girls' inability to to develop empathy or moral understanding. Looking back on this idea, it feels a bit controversial. I know what I meant, and when it comes to my daughters, I also know I've called that absolutely correctly. But if you're reading this, and you have autism, and you're thinking, 'I don't think that's true of me', then I'm sure you're right. If you have a family member or friend with autism and you're thinking this doesn't describe them then, again, you are most likely correct, too. But I have to believe that what I have said is true when it comes to my daughters, because Robyn and Liberty's behaviour shows they are practically incapable of empathy; they really do only see their own needs. And I am sure that this is due to the level of their autism. It's either that, or there are times when Libby is just an inconsequential violent rage monster for no reason. I'd rather go with what I said ten years ago.

Also, of all the song titles I chose for my blogs, this one was the most apt and my favourite.

BLOG POST FROM JUNE 19 2011 - WHAT A FOOL BELIEVES

Sometimes in life you have to ask yourself the Big Questions. You know, like:

If there is a God, how come there is so much pain and suffering in the world?

Is Climate Change a reality or an oft-peddled myth?

Does anybody, really and truly, understand how the financial markets work, including everyone who makes their living from said markets?

Why do people continue to watch weather reports when the weathermen don't even seem to know what the weather is like outside right now?

Why are sandwiches tastier cut into triangles rather than squares?

How did Philip Neville ever get to play for England once, never mind more than fifty times?

Oh yeah, and

What is the purpose of life? And how does that purpose relate to people with autism?

IF YOU'LL ALLOW ME A PHILOSOPHICAL MOMENT, I BELIEVE THAT OUR lives are about learning to be more loving and less selfish; that we are here to learn how to put other people's needs before our own. I believe that we are here to learn and to experience things; good and bad, positive and negative. We experience positive things that bring us joy so we know what we are striving for, but it's when we have negative experiences that we really learn about the important things in life, and those experiences make us stronger people.

To be honest, when it comes to negative experiences, I don't have much time for people who frequently lament their lot in life because things haven't turned out as they hoped. I'm not saying that we don't all have the right to have a moan; we're all human and it's good to get things off our chest once in a while. Neither am I saying that there aren't people who have earned the right to be unhappy; there are people in the world living in dire circumstances of all kinds. But one thing I am sure of is that I am not one of them.

As you may be aware, I am a high school teacher. I remember an occasion, a few years ago now, where a teacher was absent and I had to cover her BTEC Child Care lesson (and people say that we don't do enough academic subjects anymore...). I don't remember all the details, but the class was watching a documentary about the parents of a young child who had some illness or other. He would be able to have an operation to cure him when he was older, but for now they had to give him injections each evening. What I do recall quite clearly was the attitude of the parents. The mother was in tears saying, 'I just can't wait until this nightmare is over. I can't bear hurting my son every night with needles.' The father said, 'The main question we ask ourselves is, 'Why us?''

I admit, I was not terribly sympathetic. Yes, your life may not be perfect, but you've been blessed with a child who brings joy into your life, how about focusing on that? And besides, 'Why me?' is a rubbish question on just about every level. Bad things happen to all of us at some point or other. Sadly, there are those people that live in awful circumstances all of the time but, for most of us, life is a series of peaks and troughs, swings and roundabouts. Life isn't one long fairy tale where everything is great, not for anyone. Yes, my life is made more testing by our daughters' condition but, on the other hand, I am 40 years old and I have never experienced grief of any kind. Except when George's guinea pig died. That was pretty traumatic.

To bring me back to my original point then, I believe that my varied life experiences give me the opportunity to learn; hopefully to learn to be a better person. So, if this is the case, what are my daughters here for? Clearly, their limited capacity to learn means I cannot expect them to learn moral or educational lessons in the same way that I can. The girls do learn things here and there, of course, but improved dexterity on an iPad, or knowing every word to Disney's Tangled isn't the sort of thing I had in mind when discussing the meaning of life. When it comes to matters that can be judged to be morally correct or not, we cannot expect any kind of real learning for Robyn and Liberty. Their autism means they can never learn to really love and care for others in the same way that we would hopefully expect from ourselves. If we were to judge Robyn and Libby by our own standards, then we would say they were hugely selfish. Let me be clear; they are not selfish. They just do not have any comprehension of the needs of other people. My daughters only really understand attending to their own needs; that's the nature of the beast(s).

So, to ask the question again, what are Robyn and Liberty

here for? What is the purpose of their life? To me, it's quite simple.

I am a student in this life; I am here to learn.

Robyn and Liberty are educators; they are here to teach.

I wrote recently about my son, George, and I honestly believe that his life is richer for being raised in a house with autism at its very heart.

And me? I have no doubt that taking care of my daughters has helped me to be a better man. I am sure I am twice the man I would ever have been without them. And what does it mean to be a man? I'm not entirely sure, but I know I am never more manly than I when I am cooking, cleaning, hair brushing, tickling, singing, snuggling, toileting, soothing, dancing, fixing, dressing, washing, and generally caring for my girls. I believe their purpose is to make me a better person and I never doubt how well they achieve it.

I am disappointed on occasion when I see people denying themselves the opportunity to care for the girls. Let there be no doubt, anyone who declines to spend time with my daughters is considerably poorer for doing so. They are little rays of sunshine, true enough. But spend a little time with them and they will also make you a better person.

I believe I know my place in the world and, just as importantly, I believe I know Robyn and Liberty's place in the world, too.

PRESENT DAY

1 in 2 marriages end in divorce but, apparently, when you introduce autistic children into that mix, then the figures rise to 4 marriages in 5 ending in divorce. That's a statistic that I've read more than once. I'm not sure where that research would come

from, and I'm sufficiently capable of critical thinking to question the veracity of that statistic. However, from my own experience of people I know, and from anecdotal evidence, there is a strong suggestion that the divorce rate does seem higher in families where there is an autistic child. And that may be one child with autism, not two children who have the severity of autism that Libby and Robyn have. And yet, here we are, Karen and me, closing in on our 30th anniversary. How have we managed that?

Karen visited the school where I used to teach a few years ago. She met some of my colleagues, including my good friend Shelley, with whom I have had many discussions about the girls. 'I just wanted to tell you you're amazing', Shelley told Karen. Karen thanked her and we moved on, not thinking too much about it. The next school day, Shelley came up to me with her hands on her face. 'What was I going on about to Karen?' she said, and then put on a silly voice to emphasise what she felt was the stupidity of what she had said, '"I just wanted to tell you you're amaaaazing!" Karen must have thought I was a right idiot!'

I then had to explain to Shelley that, actually, Karen wouldn't have blinked when being told that she was amazing in regard to the girls. Ridiculous as it seems, people tell us what a fantastic job we do all the time, and such compliments aren't a big deal to us. Just like insults can be water off a duck's back, after a while, frequent compliments can be greeted in the same way. People without the mixed blessing that is additional needs kids in their lives often look at us and see something that they don't feel they could cope with. But are we 'amazing'? And what about that other thing that people often say, that we must be special parents to be given such special children?

Respectfully, there's nothing particularly special about Karen and me. We're decent people, we try our best and we love our kids, but that describes many parents. What I think is more true is that we were given a difficult situation to deal with. As I said in my blog back in the day, I believe Robyn and Libby are here to teach those around them to be better people, and that applies to us as parents. We are not 'amazing'. We have had two of the best life coaches we could ever have asked for living in our home 24/7 for twenty years. They have taught us to be better parents and better people. People often say, meaning well, 'I could never do what you do.' Our response is always the same. 'Yes, you could. If this happened to you, then you would just deal with it the best you could. What would your alternative be?'

I can appreciate that raising kids with additional needs puts extra strain on the relationship between their parents, so we shouldn't be surprised that there are additionally high rates of divorce and break ups in those relationships. Our marriage remained strong because we didn't use our girls as an excuse to put our relationship on the back burner. I'm a big believer that the most important thing we could do for our three children was to take care of each other. Our parents and other family and friends were generous with their time and their allotted amount of patience, by watching the girls for us so we could go out on dates and even, once in a while, get away for an overnight stay. And we always remembered to just be kind to each other, whenever we could. It wasn't always easy, and our relationship is not perfect, but the strength of our marriage comes from the care we take with our relationship, and that relationship is strengthened by our daughters who help us to be stronger, kinder, better people.

Our family photos aren't like other family's photos. Instead of
pinning Robyn down, she was allowed to run around here, and we
made that a feature of the photo

IT'S NICE TO HAVE A FRIEND - FAMILY & FRIENDS

BLOG POST FROM JUNE 6 2011 - LET'S HEAR IT FOR THE BOY

O*K, pop quiz, hotshot. How many children do I have? If you are either family or friend, this is obviously easy, but if not, you could possibly get the answer wrong. The answer is 3.*

Clearly, I have my two lovely autistic daughters, Robyn and Liberty. But some of you will have noticed references here and there to my lovely non-autistic son, George. George is our eldest, two years older than Robyn and is as 'normal' as any other neurotypical fifteen year-old. He likes video games, messaging on Facebook and his Blackberry, watching sitcoms, and hanging out with his friends. George's life is one of swings and round-abouts; there are times when he doesn't get our full attention and his needs take a back seat. However, as parents we try to balance this out by ensuring he gets special attention at other times. We feel we need to do this in order to compensate for the girls unavoidably taking up so much of our time.

George is a sensitive boy and a good brother to his sisters, though I think he could do even better. I've told him that this will benefit him; when girls see him taking care of his sisters they are just going to think he's the world's sweetest guy and want to take him home to meet their mother immediately. But, when push comes to shove, he has always shown his caring side where his sisters are concerned. When Robyn was a little younger and our security procedures were not as tight, she used to go missing on a fairly regular basis. George would always help us find her, and would always get upset as well in case we didn't. This was something I always found heartbreaking on top of my stress at trying to find Robyn. Bad times.

Robyn is in George's class at church and I know I can now leave him to look after her. George is a little older and more mature now, and Robyn is much more calm and placid than she used to be. She will happily sit there, ignoring the teacher and watching Toy Story 3 on her iPad, while George keeps her supplied with Wotsits, Refresher chew bars and Schweppes lemonade. I don't know how much of a distraction she is to George or the other kids in the class, but I'd like to think that looking after Robyn teaches them something in practical terms about loving those around you, whilst the teacher is only expounding the theory.

Just recently George has discovered a new way to bond with Liberty. Libby has often shown an interest in computer games, but sometimes lacks the necessary understanding to play them properly. There is an old Disney Tarzan game George has for his Nintendo DS handheld; Libby's pretty good at playing it, but inevitably she gets stuck from time to time. She brings it to Mum and Dad but ends up walking away from us chanting the mantra that she always hears in these circumstances: 'Ask George, ask George, ask George…'. Big brother is the one to sort out her video games; Mum and Dad haven't got a clue. Libby now has sufficient understanding to be able to play Mario Bros. on the Nintendo Wii, too. The great thing about this is that you can play with several players, which means the family video games oracle can play alongside her and get her through the tricky bits. I don't think George realises how heartwarming it is for us just to see *two of our children playing together, doing something as ordinary as guiding Mario and Luigi through their different levels.*

George and Libby getting their Super Mario on

The girls can benefit George, too. For his speaking assignment in his English class last year he prepared a speech and PowerPoint presentation about Robyn and Liberty that could have been called 'The pros and cons of growing up in a house with autism at its heart'. This was a winner for George as he was able to speak with confidence about a subject he knew well, and also use lots of impressive vocabulary as he spoke about 'diagnosis', 'autistic spectrum' and 'social and communication disorder'. He also got to tell some amusing stories and use that great picture of Robyn on the roof of our house. George got the only Level 7 of his scholastic career for his speech, so well done, Gee.

Our trip to Disneyland is the only 'typical' family holiday George has been on, though there was nothing typical about it. However, you shouldn't feel too sorry for him in regard to vacation time. When I was his age I'd never been on a plane, but

George has been to the USA four times: three times to see his cousins in North Carolina, and once just a couple of years ago with his Mum and Dad. His trip with us came after I promised our 4 year-old Spiderman fan that I would take him to see where Peter Parker lived when he was older. We had a great time on our trip to New York, and it was four whole days without having to worry about Robyn escaping or Libby drawing on the walls.

As Robyn and Liberty stay over at a residential centre for kids with autism on Wednesday and Thursdays during term time, and Wednesdays are George's church youth night, Thursday nights are our 'George Time'. We don't always do something special, but we do try to do something where we spend quality time with him. We often go out for dinner, but sometimes we'll just watch some TV and eat treats. Whatever we do, we all enjoy a little peace and quiet and are able to relax and not constantly have to check what George's sisters are up to. Thursday night is the new Friday night in our house.

Finding a balance between taking care of the needs of all of our children isn't easy. A lot of the time the girls come first;

there's just no avoiding it. There are many experiences that I'm sure George has missed out on by being born into a family like ours; so many things that we don't get to do that typical families take for granted. But, all things considered, I don't think he does too badly. He gets to do things and have the kind of one on one parental attention that lots of other kids don't, and he has learned to be more understanding and caring than most kids will ever be. His upbringing has been underpinned by the principle of taking care of those less fortunate than himself, and I don't think there is anything much more valuable that we could have taught him.

Anyway, I need to finish this now. I'm off to get tickets for X-Men First Class for George and me. Well, it's important to have a little quality father and son time, don't you think?

PRESENT DAY

As George got older, we realised he could be trusted to look after the girls on his own. Their behaviour was no longer as outrageous as it had been in their younger years and, as long as they had access to their tech and toys and had their food on hand, they could easily be watched by someone like George who knew them and understood what they were likely to need.

There was a large church meeting for all the congregations in the area one Sunday and, because of our church responsibilities, Karen and I both needed to be there if possible. George agreed to be on 'babysitting' duty, and as he didn't have to get up and get ready for church, he rolled out of bed when we were leaving and chilled on the settee for a while before worrying about what tasks he had to undertake that morning.

A little while into the meeting I was approached by George's friend, Alex, with his phone. He said that it was George on the line and it was an emergency. I took the phone and left the audi-torium where the meeting was being held so I could take the call. The conversation went something like this:

Me: Hey, G. Everything OK?

George: (Clearly worried and upset). No, Dad. Robyn's miss-ing. I've been looking for half an hour for her, I've been every-where, I've been searching the fields, the streets...

Me: George, George, stop. It's OK. It's OK. Robyn isn't there. She's here with us. We brought her with us this morning so you only had Libby to look after.

WHAT I HEARD NEXT WAS THE SOUND OF SOMEONE JUST EMOTIONALLY crumble. George just immediately began sobbing softly on the phone. I've never heard anything so heartbreaking in my life. I understood that reaction completely because I have cried the very same tears. Tears of pain, of relief, of guilt, of pent up emotion. You see, although Libby couldn't behave well at church, Robyn was usually pretty good, as long as she had her own treats and entertainment. It didn't seem right to leave George with both girls when Robyn probably wouldn't be much trouble for us. But we obviously didn't communicate that to George, and he was a bit sleepy when we left, so he didn't pick up on the fact that we had taken Robyn with us.

So, a little while later, when he figured it was time to just check on the girls to see if they were OK, he could only find Libby. Then would have followed the initial search for Robyn, followed by the increasing concern, but the feeling that she must be here somewhere. Then the wider search of the garden and the field, and the streets, becoming increasingly frantic. Then the awful thoughts start creeping into your mind that she is lost, gone, who knows where and with who; that something awful could be happening to her, and it's happening because you weren't taking care of her properly. And then, a dreadful but inevitable moment of making a phone call to tell your parents that you've lost your sister and you've got no idea where she is. Imagine all of that, and then imagine that it was all in vain. That she was never with you in the first place. Everything you had just experienced, some of the most harrowing minutes in your life, was for nothing. Robyn was happily eating Skittles while watching her iPad with Mum and Dad.

A more recent photo of G

I'll never forget that sound of sobbing on the other end of the phone. Poor George. Even though it was a case of 'all's well that ends well', I was devastated for him. Robyn had famously gone missing on my watch and I had to make that call to my wife, only I really had lost her. George hadn't actually lost her at all. But, emotionally, he had been through the same horrific experience. And maybe the only thing worse than going through a dreadful emotional experience is having to see your kids go through the same thing.

BLOG POST FROM JUNE 26 2011 - WITH A LITTLE HELP FROM MY FRIENDS

I am sitting in the kids' playroom in our good friends Kate & Spike's house. I have not been able to find sufficient quiet time to write this weekend, but strangely, given that we are here for Kate & Spike's new baby Esme's blessing and the house is full of people, Robyn and I have found a quiet space for her to play with the iPad, and for me to write this week's instalment. So, as I sit here, I am reminded of the many fun things that have happened in this house over the years with our girls.

Esme's blessing took place at 10am at the church, which is very close to Kate & Spike's home. There are three separate sessions of our church services, which take a lengthy three hours in total, finishing at 1pm. We made it to 10.20am before the girls behaviour meant we had to leave, which, all things considered, was quite good for Liberty.

Karen and I were not very reverent during the opening prayer. Sitting on the back row, we had supplied the girls with their usual electronic entertainment and headphones, and also plied them with sweets. Up to now, the burble of low volume conversation and prelude music had disguised any noises they might have made. But as the congregation fell deathly silent for the prayer, there was the unmistakable and suddenly loud sound of heavily slurped sweets and the secondhand hiss of Disney's Hercules leaking through headphones. Our response? Barely stifled laughter. In fairness, we don't just sit there laughing in these situations.

There is always a mad scramble to get the volume down as quickly as possible, which in turn will create a bit of a scuffle as the girls resist their volume being adjusted. All of this goes on while the congregation sit in otherwise silence as someone is up at the pulpit praying to the Almighty.

Anyway, back to the house I am sitting in. There are lots of little incidents that have happened here, as we used to stay here often before we scaled back our visits to people's houses on account of the many disasters that were experienced. I just asked Kate if she could remember any stories from our visits to their place. I remembered some of the same ones as she did, but there were others I'd forgotten that she remembered. Like Robyn's unique take on showering one Sunday morning.

Robyn enjoys her shower time, and often lies down in the bath to just let the water splash over her. It would seem that the only thing wrong with this situation for Robyn is that the hard plastic bath isn't the most comfortable of places to relax. But Kate was still surprised when she went back into the bathroom to find that Robyn had got out of the shower, gone to one of the bedrooms, dragged herself a quilt from one of the beds, wrapped herself in it and climbed back into the shower. Much more comfortable I'm sure you'll agree. There are these social conventions that we all follow, that Robyn and Libby don't give two hoots for. Wrapping yourself in a quilt so your lie down in the shower can be more comfortable? We would see that as a bit self-indulgent. It's creating a huge amount of work and effort for someone else to dry later; but why would Robyn care about that?

Another social convention that Robyn didn't care too much for in her younger years was that stuffy nonsense about wearing clothes in public. But given that she was only little, and we were at the house of good friends, this shouldn't be such a big deal. Then one day there was one of those knocks at the door that we get from time to time, even when we're at someone else's house.

It was a neighbour of Kate & Spike's, wondering if we knew that the little girl who was visiting here had escaped and was now running at speed away from the house. Stark naked. The escaping part is the dangerous and worrying bit. The naked bit is just the additional dose of humiliation you get as you chase down the road after her, passing the good people of Runcorn, sitting in their front gardens on a lovely day, wondering who the rather strange, squealing, naked kid is running past their house.

Some stories are funny at the time, some become funny afterwards when you're retelling the tale. We were getting ready to leave Kate & Spike's one Sunday evening having stayed for the weekend. We gathered bags and coats and were about to start saying our farewells, with all of us in the lounge or the conservatory that is adjacent to the lounge. Often these kinds of incidents come about because you've had to go into another room, or you've been distracted for a minute or two. The troubling thing about this incident was that Robyn nearly died within a couple of feet of four adults. She was walking around the low windowsill in the conservatory that went all the way around the room. This is the kind of thing that Robyn loves to do, walking on low walls and sills, getting to the end and walking back. As she was walking along the thin windowsill, she slipped. As she slipped she managed to hook her head in the loop of the cord that pulled the blinds up and down. I looked up to see that Robyn had totally fallen from the sill and was hanging in this 'noose', quickly turning deep purple. It was over in a few seconds, and she wasn't badly injured, but the scar around her neck was a reminder for the next few months of what sometimes happens with Robyn's athleticism, even when you've barely turned your back.

So, something a little lighter to finish? Spike works in the Audio Visual business and, as you would, has a very nice AV set up with an amp and speakers for the television in their lounge. And given that he gets his AV equipment at knockdown prices, you would imagine correctly that these speakers could really pack a punch. Our wives had gone out shopping and left us home with the kids, so Spike, George and I were chatting in the dining room, and Libby decided that while we were out of the living room she would put a DVD on. This in itself wasn't a problem, but while putting it on she decided to press a few buttons and turn a few dials on the amp. One of the things she had done was to turn the powerful amp and speakers up to full volume. Then the DVD came on and, as luck would have it, she chose a DVD released by top film studio Metro Goldwyn Mayer. As always happens at the start of a film from this studio, the MGM lion roared, only this was now at house shaking volume turned all the way up to 11. I simultaneously thought I was having heart failure and that we were about to experience some sort of low scale 9/11 with a plane about to crash into the house. Frightening for a moment, but quickly quite funny.

The amazing thing is, after all of these and many other little incidents that have happened, Kate & Spike are still our dearest friends. They obviously need to get out a bit more and meet people. There's got to be lower maintenance friends than us knocking about, surely?

Christmas celebrations with Kate, Spike and their kids

PRESENT DAY

Liberty also likes to apply her love of the movies to family friends. For reasons that are sometimes obvious but sometimes best known to her, people occasionally get a nickname bestowed upon them that Libby has borrowed from a film. So, as an obvious example, a friend called Sarah is 'Aunt Sarah', not in that way that kids do where they call a close family friend uncle or aunt, but simply because there is a character in Disney's Lady & The Tramp who is called Aunt Sarah. Another nickname dates back to one night at a church activity, when Libby was wearing her green coat and Robyn was wearing her red coat. Then Libby noticed that our friend Carrie was wearing a blue hoodie. Libby made Robyn and Carrie line up with her to take a photo. Why? Because red, blue and green are the colours of the outfits worn by the good fairies in Disney's Sleeping Beauty. She likes to look at the photo and point to each of them in turn saying the fairies' names: 'Flora, Fauna, Merryweather!' Needless to say, Carrie is now forever known as Merryweather whenever Libby is around.

Carrie, Libby & Robyn. Flora, Fauna & Merryweather

Rachel is a family friend who has always taken a special

interest in our girls, especially Libby, ever since she was given an assignment to look after her at church. Libby gave Rachel the monicker of Ginger; not because Rachel has ginger hair or likes to eat ginger biscuits, but because there is a character in the Aardman animated movie Chicken Run played by Julia Sawalha called Ginger. Karen and I were chatting with Rachel about this the other night, but none of us can remember quite when and how Rachel became Ginger, which is a shame and, on reflection, seems a little odd, given that Ginger is, of course, a chicken, and Rachel does not resemble a chicken in any way. Still, it's definitely affectionately meant, otherwise Rachel would have been called Mrs Tweedy, the Chicken Run baddie.

BLOG POST FROM SEPTEMBER 3 2011 - ANIMAL

A few years ago, ITV, a British TV channel, aired a drama called After Thomas starring Keeley Hawes. It was the story of a family consisting of two parents and their son Kyle, who had autism. I found out about it the next day when everyone else watched it and asked us if we had seen it, too. 'No', we replied, 'why didn't you tell us it was on?' It seems my media awareness means everyone assumes I know when anything interesting is on TV. No-one thought a quick courtesy call to see if we were watching was a good idea.

I remembered about the programme recently, and decided to look to see if it was available on DVD. I managed to find it after a quick search online, so I bought it for Karen and me to watch with George on a family night in. The film told the story of how Kyle overcame aspects of his autism, including much of his aggression, when the family bought a dog, which they used both as therapy and to help Kyle communicate. I enjoyed After Thomas at the time, but I cannot bear the stupid thing now. You see, Libby also chose to sit down and watch it with us, which is surprising considering that it wasn't animated or even particularly kid friendly. Perhaps she spotted a kindred spirit in Kyle.

In fact, Liberty liked it so much that she hunted down clips of After Thomas to watch on YouTube, which she watched repeatedly. The thing was, Libby's favourite scenes were the ones in which Kyle was having huge tantrums in public. Libby thought this was hilarious. Now, dealing with a public meltdown from your autistic offspring can be enormously challenging. However, you are helped by the fact that you love this child and, sometimes at least, those strong feelings help you to keep your temper under control as you do your best to help them overcome their frustration. When a kid is having a meltdown in a film, all you have is the irritation of the awful noise this kid is making, without any feelings of compassion because it's just acting; it isn't even real. After a while my catchphrase became, 'No Kyle, Libby!' The very sound of listening to this kid going faux nuts just set me on edge. She was only allowed to watch it with a decent pair of headphones on.

This is a rather long introduction to this post's theme of the girls' experiences with animals. Possibly because of After Thomas, my mother and others have often suggested that we get a dog as it might help the girls to make progress. Whilst the idea has merit, the response to this suggestion is always, 'No'. I am quite aware how outrageously harsh this sounds, but we've already got a couple of characters in the house that we have to feed, wash and take for walks. Plus they have a tendency to wreck the place (like the dogs we had growing up) and we often have to clean up wee and poo from inappropriate places, too. The girls might enjoy a dog, but we've got our hands full already, thank you.

My mum and dad have always kept dogs, and going over to their house to take their dog Molly for a walk is a favourite activity for us. Robyn is entrusted with holding Molly's lead and she responsibly walks her along the streets, until we reach the country park near mum and dad's where we can let her off her lead (Molly, not Robyn). There was a nice moment with Robyn and Molly recently when mum brought the dog over to our house. As Molly crouched under the table, Robyn got on all fours to go nose to nose with her. It was a lovely scene as dog and daughter checked each other over, and I don't doubt Robyn would enjoy having a dog around the house. Liberty is less keen, and often reacts as if she is afraid of Molly when we arrive at mum's house, though she seems to get over this quickly.

A frosty morning walk with my Mum's dog Molly, with George, Robyn & Libby

Robyn does seem to have a way with animals in general, actually. As I have told you previously, the land that backs onto our house is a grazing field for cows. Robyn has been known to sit on our side of the chain link fence and beckon the cows to her. They all cease chewing the cud and crowd round her as she makes her autistic noises, seeming to have them under her spell. We call her 'The Cow Whisperer'. When we go over towards the cows, they all quickly walk away. The cows seem to sense something with Robyn; possibly a complete absence of fear and someone who would never deliberately harm them. I best not tell the cows how often Robyn likes to tuck into their friends when she goes to Mcdonald's, though.

Not all creatures have fared as well at Robyn's hands, however. I sat down one time to find I was sitting on something that wasn't there a minute ago. It turned out to be a dead bird that Robyn had brought in from the garden for me, as if she were a cat. I've always hoped that she found it dead to begin with, rather than her being a bird killer. Finishing creatures off is not beyond her abilities.

We tried having pets a few years ago when we bought George a guinea pig called Neo. Unfortunately, Neo was the runt of his litter and quite weak; he wasn't with us for very long before he died. To help George overcome his grief at losing Neo, my mum bought him a new guinea pig the next day; a much livelier fellow that he called Scamper. We covered the frame of an old divan bed that Robyn had destroyed in chicken wire, to use as a run for Scamper to play in (the bed was broken by Robyn's constant jumping on it and tipping it upside down – another story entirely). It was an ingenious idea; plenty of space for the little guy to run about whilst keeping him perfectly safe from preda-tors. It was also light enough to move around different areas of the garden. It turns out this last bit was a major design flaw, though. One afternoon, Robyn decided to give Scamper a bit more freedom and lifted the bed frame up to allow him to escape. He ran into the field via next-door's garden and we never saw Scamper again. Poor fella.

One summer, Robyn kept coming into the house with her hands seemingly covered in wallpaper paste. The paste was clear, gooey and thick, but was also quite difficult to wash off her hands. It had to be scraped off, rather than it rinsing off with warm water and soap. We had no idea where she was getting *this viscous substance from, just that she quite often returned from the garden with her hands covered in the stuff. Eventually we watched her playing outside and found the source of the 'wallpaper paste'. Whenever Robyn found a slug in the garden, she picked it up and literally squeezed the life out of it until it exploded in her hands. We were not so keen to volunteer for the job of washing her hands after we had found out that the paste was actually slug innards. Top tip, though; if you're decorating the house and you ever find yourself running low on wallpaper paste...*

Robyn and Grandy take Jenny for a walk

❧ 11 ❧
BACK TO DECEMBER -
CHRISTMAS
PRESENT DAY

Having ground to a halt in August of 2011, I decided, in the best tradition of British sitcoms, to bring the blog back for a couple of Christmas specials. Quite simply, there were stories to tell about Christmas, and it made far more sense to post those as we approached the festive season, rather than in September. Also, Christmas has been the backdrop of some important family stories. There was the Christmas morning in 2000 that I've already talked about, with Robyn and the Teletubbies. And there was another one that was completely unrelated to autism the following year when Karen went into hospital on Christmas Eve with a heart virus. And then there was the annual Christmas plotting and planning to try to get Robyn to actually participate in some way...

BLOG POST FROM DECEMBER 6 2011 - ALL I WANT FOR CHRISTMAS IS YOU

I love Christmas. Always have. It's a family time, a spiritual time, a time of peace, a time of love, a time of giving and, let's be honest, a time of indulgence. It's different from every other day of the year; we do things that we don't do at any other time, and this is partly what makes it exciting for children and nostalgic for adults. We add new decorations to our homes, new lighting and new smells from fragrant candles. We eat different food, we move our furniture around and bring trees and shrubberies indoors and put lights on them. When you think of the day itself we do very few of the mundane things we do on other days, and we indulge in ceremonies like the opening of presents and the carving of the roast beast! As the song says, it really is the most wonderful time of the year, precisely because everything is so different. The normal world gets put on hold for a few days whilst we indulge in this festive fantasy.

Now imagine that your ability to deal with the everyday world depends entirely on things being kept the same. Imagine that the world only makes sense when a pattern of order is followed. And then, one day, let's call it Christmas Day, your whole world gets turned upside down. Everything you expect to happen, doesn't happen, and everything that happens is not what you expect. How do you deal with that?

I'll tell you how. You shut yourself away and pretend none of it is happening. You ignore it completely and just try to do what you always do. We have camcorder footage of Christmases gone by, and the reaction of our children couldn't be more different. A young George, on entering the room on Christmas Day, falls to his knees in awe like the shepherds and wise men in the stable in Bethlehem did 2,000 years ago. Although, their awe was due to being in the presence of the Saviour of mankind, rather than just being in the presence of a ruckload of gifts. But, you know, he was pretty excited. The video also shows Robyn walking into the room, walking straight past the piles of presents and straight out of the other door, closing it behind her. She wasn't interested in what we were doing with those presents, she just wanted to get herself on the other side of the door to put that distance between her and Christmas.

In the years that followed, we tried really hard to do things for Robyn that we thought she might enjoy so we could get her to stay in the room with us and be a part of our family Christmas morning. One year, we bought her a Disney Princess camp chair with cup holders that held a new cup with a curly straw with a serving of her beloved Pepsi and a packet of her favourite crisps of the time (Nice 'n' Spicy Nik-Naks – good choice!). It didn't work.

Another year we bought an indoor play tent and put all of Robyn's presents inside in the hope that this would pique her interest, but to no avail. I remember a Christmas morning where I'd bought her Toy Story 1&2 on DVD to get her interested in opening presents. I gave her this gift first and managed to get her sufficiently interested in it to unwrap it, and she was suitably pleased with the contents. So pleased, in fact, that she took it into the next room, put the film in the DVD player, shut the door, and refused to come out for several hours until she was entirely convinced that we were done with the whole present unwrapping thing. If any of us entered the room (say, to go through into the kitchen), she would dart to the door to shut it behind us. For Robyn, Christmas had to be kept out at all costs.

After a while we learned not to expect anything but disdain from Robyn on Christmas morning. When we had the extension to our house built it meant an additional Christmas bonus for her. It meant on Christmas morning Robyn could walk past the Christmas presents in the lounge, into the dining room, close the door behind her, then walk into the new playroom and close that *door behind her, too. That way she was two whole rooms and two closed doors away from all of that Christmas nonsense.*

What we realised in time was that trying to make things 'special' for Robyn actually just made things worse. What she was rejecting was the whole 'differentness' of the day. Making her a special breakfast of Pepsi and crisps and building special tents just made an already different and difficult day even more unusual and distasteful for Robyn. We accepted defeat and resigned ourselves to the fact that Robyn was never going to join in on Christmas morning. We gave up wrapping presents for her; what was the point? She might be interested in the items eventually, but she wasn't interested in going through the rigmarole of opening complicated wrapping, and she certainly wasn't interested in them on Christmas morning. Here was yet another special family occasion that had become a casualty of autism in our home.

And then, as if being rewarded by the gods of autism for our willingness to accept Robyn's fear of Christmas, we were given December 25th 2010. Finally, after years of toil and trial, we were blessed with our very own little Christmas miracle. It seemed as though Robyn could actually deal with Christmas morning if we just left her alone and didn't try quite so hard. I think it was also possible that, in a weird way, Christmas had become part of a routine for her. Robyn now seemed to accept that, once every 365 days, we had this one day that was very different to all the others, and actually, if she could get past the differentness, it turned out to be dead good. If she could turn a blind eye to all the ceremony of the day, her reward was more Disney Princess merchandise than she could shake a rather large stick at. She knew that when we started to put lights, trees and decorations up in the house that we'd soon have that odd day with all the presents. So, last Christmas morning we watched in surprise and wonder as our three children sat together and opened presents. We didn't know whether to laugh or cry.

So, those of you with neurotypical children, as you watch your children sit together, opening gifts like it's the most natural thing in the world and taking your generosity for granted, remember to be quietly grateful. Some of us have waited years to see that happen, and some of us have not seen it happen yet. Whether or not we will get a repeat performance this year or not, I do not know. But I do know there is nothing I can do to make it happen either way. As always with autism, acceptance is required to find the peace within. Even at Christmas.

All our children opening Christmas presents together

BLOG POST FROM DECEMBER 18 2011 - WHEN CHRISTMAS COMES TO TOWN

Robyn and Libby with their new pyjamas on
Christmas Eve

Last time out I told you about how, until last year at least, my daughter Robyn totally rejected anything to do with Christmas. From reading this you could be forgiven for thinking that all children with autism hate Christmas, but it isn't necessarily the case. From what I have read, a loathing of Christmas due to the complete disruption it causes is not uncommon among children with autism, but there is also twinkling lights and excitement to stimulate the senses, and some autistic kids really enjoy this. In our house, there is a 50/50 split in attitude towards Christmas amongst our autistic offspring. Robyn hates it. Liberty absolutely loves it, possibly enough for both of them.

For Libby, Christmas starts as soon as possible. If she gets a sniff of the festive season in October, then she's all over it; she starts singing Christmas songs and doesn't stop until about April. She watches The Snowman all year round. We decorate our house, minus the main tree, in early December, and as Libby walks around the place she regards her environment with wondering awe. She can't resist handling the figures in the Nativity and gazing longingly at the twinkling lights.

But before we get to Christmas Day, we first have to nego-tiate Christmas Eve. It's a day where we have to make sure we get out with the girls as we know they're likely to be mostly cooped up in houses over Christmas and Boxing Day. Of course, the British weather means that outdoor activities are often ruled out so, in their younger years at least, we would take them to one of those indoor play centres that go by the name of something like Wacky Warehouse, Jungle Gym or Chucky Cheese's – it seems you can call them what you like as long as the phrase uses alliteration.

The problem with these places as a destination for our pre-Christmas workout for the girls is that not many other parents take their kids to them on Christmas Eve. With our autistic girls, that may not seem like a problem, but it is. It seems these other people are probably too busy with Christmas preparations and know they can get their kids to be good at home by threatening them with letting Father Christmas know they've misbehaved. Christmas Eve is never a good day for kids to upset the big fella. But that threat doesn't really cut much ice in our house. So, because their indoor playhouse business is not very busy and the workers themselves have plenty to do in their own homes, they have a tendency to close early. We were caught out by this one year, as they were already closed when we got there, despite the fact that it was a good couple of hours before the official closing time. This meant that we had to find some other place for the girls to expend some energy on a rainy Christmas Eve; not easily done.

The following year we called ahead to see if they were staying open until the official closing time and they assured us that they were. When we arrived though, they tried to turn us away because they had decided to close early after all. Karen and I are not the kind of people who complain about service in restaurants or shops; we're just not pushy people. However, we were prepared to make an exception for someone who was *about to ruin our Christmas by not allowing the girls to have their last mad run around before the beginning of the festivities. We told them we'd called ahead, we had special needs children who needed to use their facilities and we weren't going away. They asked if we minded if they clean up and vacuum the place while the kids played. We were more than happy for them to do so as long as they let us in, and this meant that George, Robyn and Liberty had the run of the entire place, and after an hour or so they were thoroughly sweaty and tired. Which is the whole idea.*

In our preparations for this Christmas, Liberty has started to do something that reminded me of myself growing up. When I was quite young I liked to go snooping in my parents' room for Christmas presents that they might have bought for me, although I learned after a while that knowing what presents you were going to get made Christmas morning a bit rubbish. In fact, I actively avoid finding any presents in our room these days, and I still don't like it if I inadvertently stumble upon something that Karen's bought me for Christmas, as it has spoilt my surprise. But, this Christmas, like her Dad back in the 70s, Libby has learned to snoop. Karen and I have had to remember to keep our bedroom door locked shut at all times or bad things can happen.

A couple of weeks ago, someone left the bedroom door open not long after we'd had a special delivery from Disney.- co.uk. The box was a veritable treasure trove of Disney goodies, all of which were for the girls on Christmas morning. The trouble was, once Liberty had seen them, there was no way of explaining to her that she wasn't allowed to have them until Christmas Day – that's a concept she just can't understand*. She gets impatient waiting for her popcorn to pop in the microwave, so there's no chance of her getting her head around the idea of waiting three or four weeks for a present she knows is on the other side of the door right now! It was a hellish morning for us as Libby went nuts at least every five minutes to try and get into our bedroom to get her hands on those presents. So, when she was out with her care workers that afternoon, Karen wrapped them up and hid them in the loft. Once we could take Libby into our room and she could no longer see the Disney toys, she was happy to forget about it. The beauty of it is this; on Christmas morning it will be like she's never seen these presents before, and she'll gasp in awe in that wonderfully over dramatic way of hers that she copies from the movies she watches.

We eat Christmas dinner at my Mum and Dad's house, and it's a big traditional affair. Most of our family that live in this country, probably about 25 of us, gather around a huge table for roast beef (we've never understood why the most important meal of the year is celebrated with turkey, the cheapest, driest meat there is, so we have our favourite instead) with all the trimmings (not just some of them, all of them). But Karen and I have learned to take necessary precautions if we have any intention of participating in this family celebration. Everybody else in the family may be happy to sit for hours and eat and pull crackers and tell lame jokes and wear paper hats, but the girls aren't. So Robyn takes to the festive table with an iPad with all her favourite movies on, and Libby has a laptop, both of which have headphones attached. And they don't eat roast dinners, either; instead, they have a special festive curry, which is exactly like the curry they have the rest of the year, except they're eating it on Christmas Day. We make a big pan of curry on Christmas Eve and take a couple of dishes to my Mum's for dinner, and that way they've got plenty of their favourite meal for Christmas and Boxing Day, whilst the rest of us are eating rather more traditional fare.

We are getting better every year at doing Christmas with our daughters, because it's all about handling expectations. We can't allow ourselves to think we're allowed to socialise at someone else's house for hours whilst the girls sit and behave; it's not going to happen. A number of Christmas Day celebrations in the past have ended prematurely, with me dragging the girls to the *car and taking them home where I brood for the rest of the day, wondering why I'm left sitting on my own at home while the rest of the world seems to get to spend quality time with their nearest and dearest.*

So, Christmas dinner now starts with a phone call from my mum to let me know exactly when the Christmas dinner is going to land on the table, which is served up with curry and gadgets for the girls. And if I can manage to sit and chat with my family for half an hour after dinner without the girls kicking off completely, I can consider the day a success. As long as expectations about what kind of day we're going to have are reigned in, I can settle down on Christmas evening and watch Doctor Who with a tin of Quality Street chocolates and a glass of Vimto and ginger ale, entirely happy with my Christmas, knowing my girls are happy, too.

*Libby's lack of understanding about waiting for Christmas came before her understanding of calendars. This has helped enormously with such situations.

PRESENT DAY

Libby is still as mad about Christmas as ever, and Robyn, strangely, has definitely started to love it a little, too. This year I've caught her listening to Christmas music on her iPad quite a few times.

Libby has become more organised with her expectations about presents. She's very good at browsing the internet and she often comes across things she fancies. She understands the idea that you can't just have expensive presents all the time for no reason, so anything she sees that she likes the look of gets added to her present list that she keeps updated in her head. Anything she sees after Christmas goes on the birthday list (Libby's birthday is in October), anything between birthday and Christmas goes on the Christmas list. What tends to happen is, with ten months to wait until her birthday, her present list gets so long that we have to explain to her that some of the items will need to go on her Christmas list, and she's usually OK with that.

Further evidence that Robyn has started to enjoy
Christmas

Libby has a great memory, and she repeatedly recites her list to us, possibly to make sure we don't forget, probably because she just likes saying her list out loud. Her list is often a short speech with description, and it never varies, other than to some-times add more things to the list. One from the recent past that I heard many, many times goes something like this: 'Christmas presents. Cinderella 2015, Cinderella in blue ball gown for the royal ball, the doll, Lady Tremaine in green and black, the doll, Fairy Godmother with magical wand, the doll, Cinderella and the Prince, the dolls, on their wedding day! Gelli Baff.'

Gelli Baff is a powder that you add to a bath to turn the bath water into colourful goo. Libby loves Gelli Baff and this is always at the end of her present list. Whatever special occasion is being celebrated, Libby expects a couple of boxes of Gelli Baff thrown in. It's the law.

Libby with a new stash of Gelli Baff

Something that has become problematic with her present lists is Liberty's insistence on rediscovering older movies and deciding that she now wants to have merchandise from these classics. Those dolls from the list I just mentioned weren't cheap as they were from the more expensive 'Film Collection' from the 2015 release of Disney's live action version of Cinderella. However, they were fairly easy to get hold of as Libby asked for them around the time that the film and DVD were released, so it was simply a matter of going along to the Disney Store and handing over a fairly large wedge of cash. But when she decides that Disney's Chicken Little from 2006 is her new favourite, and she starts asking for figures and books and toys, her presents suddenly get much harder to source. Often they are only available on eBay in America and so, as well as the premium you are paying because you can't get this stuff in the shops anymore, you're paying a hefty postage fee.

A few years back she got into the DVD of Barbie and the 12 Dancing Princesses which had been released about 10 years earlier. Unsurprisingly, Libby decided that she wanted all 12 dancing princesses a long time after the fact. Every time she recited her birthday present list we'd get the full rundown of all that balletic royalty. 'Libby's birthday: Barbie and the 12 Dancing Princesses, the dolls: Barbie, Ashlyn, Blair, Courtney, Delia, Edeline, Fallon, Hadley, Isla, Janessa, Kathleen, and Lacey. Gelli Baff.' Eventually we found a seller on eBay who was selling all 12 princesses as a set, albeit not in boxes, and even came with the bonus of the doll of Prince Derek! (Derek? Derek?? In what universe do you get a prince called Derek? Other than the Barbie universe, obviously.) That little lot cost us the thick end of £150.

All 12 Barbie Dancing Princesses. And Prince Derek!

Now the girls have moved out of our home and live in their own places, the finances from their benefits are dealt with differently. If they've paid their rent and other costs and they've got some spare in the bank, then Libby and Robyn can have more or less whatever they want (not that they didn't really have that before). Among other things on Libby's current present list are a very specific bike that costs £400, and a steel wagon for her to pull around (like Matilda in the film) that is another £150. I'm not entirely convinced she's going to use either of them that much, but as long as she has the money in her account, who are we to stop her from having everything she wants?

Another Christmas Eve new pyjamas shot

❦ 12 ❦

WE ARE NEVER EVER GETTING BACK TOGETHER - FAMILY OCCASIONS

PRESENT DAY

For a long time, we did our utmost to be like a 'normal family' whenever we could. Specifically in this chapter, I am referring to days out, or attending family occasions and celebrations. We had two girls with autism that could result in some seriously anti-social behaviour, but that wasn't going to stop us doing what we would have done if they didn't have this condition. If there were weddings/baptisms/blessings/birthday parties to attend, this branch of the Dickenson family was going to be there, all present and correct. No one was going to accuse us of wimping out or using our girls as an excuse to not attend important events. Not us.

I think a lot of this was down to the way Karen and I were brought up in our family homes; it was about the example both sets of parents had set for us as children, and even after we'd grown up and left home. When Liberty was born, she arrived in the world at just before 1am on a Thursday morning, and Karen brought her home on the Thursday afternoon. At this point in time, Karen was in charge of the women's group at church, and it so happened that they had an activity planned for that Thursday evening. Anyone with an ounce of sense in this situation would either cancel the activity or ask someone else to take charge for that one night and stay at home and rest. No one would even think of criticising you for that. You've just had a baby, literally that day, for crying out loud! Just relax!

But Karen and I both come from families where you 'just get on with it'. That's how we were raised and that's what we saw time and time again from our parents. You don't make a fuss about yourself just because things aren't perfect, and if you have a responsibility then you discharge of that responsibility as well as you can, more or less regardless of the circumstances. So, of course, Karen arrived at church that night, carrying Liberty, not even a day old, in a baby's car seat, hugging, waving and smiling at everyone, ready to take charge and 'just get on with it'. Because that's what we do. Probably because we knew that's what our parents expected of us. We didn't want to be seen as lightweights who couldn't handle what life had thrown at us.

It's a bit of a double-edged sword when I look back. I am proud of how we have been able to care for our family with the minimum of fuss in circumstances that were sometimes beyond trying, and people have always been full of admiration for how we've dealt with that situation, and I suppose it pleases me that people see us as strong and capable parents. But I also look back and realise that there were plenty of times where we probably shouldn't have just got on with it. There really is no shame in swallowing your pride sometimes and just saying, 'No, we can't do that. Not right now.' It would have been OK to do that sometimes, but we rarely did. I can only speak for myself but, mentally and emotionally, I think I paid a hefty price for just getting on with it.

Our need to keep calm and carry on meant that, for a long time, we always attended family events and special occasions. There are lots of birthdays in September in our family. For that reason, we often have a get together around this time with extended family on my Mum's side. Sometimes this is held at my

Mum's house in Wrexham where we live, and sometimes it's at my aunt and uncle's in Dorridge, near Solihull. I don't know how true it is, but my sister tells me there aren't any working class areas in or around Solihull, and Dorridge certainly doesn't have any. We used to enjoy going to stay there with my aunt and uncle and our cousins in the summer when we were kids. My uncle was a policeman before he retired, so it's not like they are millionaires or anything, but they have a nice house in a nice part of the world. Just the kind of place we are always a little wary of rocking up to with Libby and Robyn.

For a while, everything went to plan. The house was very busy with guests, as you would expect at this type of family gathering. Libby was enjoying running up and down and through people's legs, and Robyn was exploring. We tried to be polite and chat to all my relatives whilst still keeping an eye on the girls, and then Robyn decided to take herself upstairs. Of course, other than trips to the bathroom, it's not good form to go exploring the upstairs rooms in someone's house when invited to a social gathering. However, a different set of rules apply to Robyn.

She found herself a bed and decided she fancied a lie down, so she just climbed in and got under the covers. True, it may be a little impolite to help yourself to a stranger's bed, but given what else she might get up to, it seemed pretty harmless. If the girls are busying themselves with something, and they're not causing anyone any trouble, then just let them get on with it. Let sleeping dogs lie. I left her to it, promising myself I would come upstairs every five to ten minutes to check everything was OK.

In fairness, that's exactly what I did. I could have stayed upstairs but, even though Robyn was allowed to break the social conventions of entering people's bedrooms, it didn't feel right for me. Also, I knew it would be seen by those close to me as just skiving a social occasion; using the girls to avoid speaking to actual human beings is my typical M.O. when we go more or less anywhere. So, I popped upstairs, checked she was OK, then went back down again, and did that on several occasions.

Looking back, I would have done things differently. Well, of course I would. If I'd known what was going to happen then we wouldn't have gone to the family gathering in the first place. And, if we really had to go, then the other thing I could have done is not left Robyn on her own for so long. Yes, I really did only leave her for around ten minutes at a time before checking on her. But I learned that ten minutes can be an awfully long time for things to go horribly wrong.

I checked on Robyn probably three or four times and she was just happily lying in her adopted bed. All good. Nothing to worry about. But, by the next time I went up, if you'll forgive my turn of phrase, the **** had seemed to literally hit the fan. It certainly looked like it had, at least. This was during Robyn's rather lengthy smearing phase, and she had chosen this very moment, whilst visiting my aunt and uncle's very lovely home in Dorridge, to poo her pants and then smear the contents of said pants absolutely everywhere; over the bedroom walls, all along the landing walls, on the carpets, on the cushions... It will be difficult for you to imagine, even if you wanted to, the sheer volume of poo, and the amount of the upstairs part of the house that she had managed to cover in so short a time. If Robyn viewed such behaviour as artistry, then this was truly her master-piece. This was like the work of Michelangelo, only with the walls of a suburban dwelling acting as her canvas rather than the ceiling of the Sistine Chapel, and working using the medium of faeces instead of paint.

I took in the scene with sheer horror. In case you're wondering, my horror was not due to disgust at the clean up job I was about to undertake. Oh gosh, no. Cleaning up walls and windows covered in crap was just a regular Tuesday for us. However, we'd learned to deal with that happening in our house through deeply unpleasant experience. We had learned to ignore odd patches of our walls that either featured suspiciously brown smears that had stubbornly refused to be moved, or patches where the paint was now missing from the walls, so vigorously had they been scrubbed in order to remove the smearing. But how to deal with this in someone else's house?

Of course, we had a great 'go to' in terms of readily available cleaning materials. Baby wipes are always your friend when you've got younger kids. And even when they've grown up you probably still keep buying them, wondering how you ever coped without them in your life. So I went to retrieve the wipes from our bag we'd brought for the girls, and surreptitiously told Karen and my Mum as I did so that their help was needed ASAP to deal with a Code Red situation. Or was that a Code Brown situation? Anyway, to continue the military metaphor, in terms of family disasters, we had reached DEFCON 1.

We immediately got to work, scooping where scooping was required, but mostly scraping and wiping. Unfortunately, such a cleaning action only serves to freshen up the smell which, obviously, was gaggingly intense, and helped it to drift downstairs. My uncle came up to survey the damage to his house and didn't say much before returning downstairs. Given what he might have said in such a situation, I thought keeping circumspect was a reasonable and thoroughly British response. We continued doing our best to turn the brown walls back to a more suitable shade of magnolia. I was also scrubbing away at a pooey cushion and not having much success, so my Mum literally took the situation out of my hands by snatching the cushion and chucking it out of the window onto the flat garage roof beneath us. I don't know if they ever found it and what they thought but, sorry about that Aunt Sue. Though, it was actually your sister's fault, that one, so talk to her about replacing it.

I don't remember how clean we got my aunt's house. It was probably far from perfect, though it wouldn't have been for the lack of trying or elbow grease. But, unlike us, my aunt and uncle will not have become accustomed to having a poo stained house, and they probably had to redecorate soon afterwards. They said nothing about what had happened, though other relatives were very consoling and assured us that it wasn't anyone's fault and we shouldn't feel bad about it. In fairness, it's easy to be understanding when it isn't your house that has been generously daubed in human excrement, but their kind words were appreciated.

As incidents involving our girls go, this was, in many ways, superficial. It was nothing that couldn't have been rectified with some proper cleaning and a lick of paint. It shouldn't have been as difficult an experience as Robyn going missing, or Libby's violent attacks that were to come along later. But, as much I've played this for laughs in my recounting of the story, there was something about this debacle that puts it high up in our All Time Top Ten of Worst Events with Robyn and Liberty. Karen was beside herself. I was deeply, deeply embarrassed. I don't think I've ever really gotten over it. I'm sure there is no real bad blood, but to this day I still feel a bit awkward at family gatherings with my Mum's side of the family and this must have happened over 10 years ago.

There were other occasions where things went badly awry, although, I'd struggle to remember them all. After a while, they just merged into one rather miserable and unsatisfying mush of big days gone wrong. We did try to make plans and preparations in order to limit the possibility of disaster. We always took toys and treats and books and, as technology progressed, music and movies on devices for the girls to listen to and watch. The girls wore headphones when listening to or watching their devices, and this meant that they could even use technology in church. The headphones helped keep them in their own little world and stopped them being distracted by their surroundings, or things like crying babies that would upset Libby, particularly. And, obviously, the headphones kept the sound in, as is appropriate whilst listening to The Clash and The Human League (some of Robyn's favourites) whilst at reverent church services.

Two of the girls' uncles and two of their aunts got married during the girls' younger years, and they attended all four of those weddings. I say 'attended', but the best we usually got was running around the corridors while the ceremony itself took place in the chapel area. When Karen's brother got married, we did our best with the usual preparations of food and entertainment. We got someone to save us a pew near the exit, which meant we could arrive as close to the start of the wedding as possible to maximise the amount of time during the service that the girls might be quiet. If the girls were good and we timed it right, we might even get to see the happy couple actually exchange their vows, which is surely what we were supposed to be there for.

Bless Robyn and Libby, they settled down quickly, got their headphones on, opened their crisps, and we waited for the bride to arrive. And waited… and waited. The girls were good as gold for 45 minutes, no mean feat given that even Robyn was only about 5 at this time. Unfortunately, all our perfect planning didn't make any difference because the bride, as is her prerogative, was 50 minutes late. So despite 45 minutes of great behaviour from the girls, we didn't see a minute of the actual wedding itself. In fact, the only one of those four wedding ceremonies that I was actually present for was Karen's sister's, and that was because I was the bishop who was actually performing the ceremony that day.

A reception at one of Karen's brother's weddings stays in my mind. Not because of the speeches or the cake or the food. I don't remember any of that. The memory I have is of trying fruitlessly to entertain Robyn in the corridor, preventing her from running around the hall where the reception was held because they were giving speeches and it wasn't the time for Robyn to be legging it around the place, practising her high pitched squealing.

What really stands out about that night is how I felt. What's the point, I asked myself time and again. Why am I here? What are we even doing this for? I'm having an absolutely rubbish time just so other people aren't disturbed by my daughters. And why are the girls here? Surely they'd much rather be some place else, too? They're getting frustrated at not being able to do what they want to do. They're getting upset. And why? So we don't offend people by not turning up. So we can get all dressed up and trot along to some event and act like a perfectly happy, typical family, when, almost guaranteed, by the end of the day, several of us would be in tears and we would all, without exception, have had a perfectly miserable time. The whole thing was a nonsense which benefitted no one.

I don't think that was the last family event we attended, but maybe this was where I really started to think that special family days were not for us. Eventually, we gave up trying to make everyone else's occasions work for our family, and everyone ended up happier for that decision being made. Karen is far more sociable than I am and actually enjoys these occasions, so the solution we came up with was that, whenever we were invited to a family celebration of some sort, she would take George with her, and I would stay at home with Robyn and Liberty. It worked out better for everyone, and it left us wondering why we'd ever bothered trying to make those days work for our family in the first place when they were so obviously going to be a complete disaster.

What had made those occasions worse, I think, was that these were supposed to be happy days. These were the days that people would always remember and reflect on. Days where all the family gathered and spent quality time together. What a great day that was! Look at the happy faces on the photos! Happy Faces? There are actual official family wedding photos with me on where I am exhibiting a face that looks like an artist's rendition of the simile 'face like thunder'. I was never happy on these occasions, because it was *supposed* to be so happy and it *always* ended up being utterly soul destroying. To have a bad day is one thing. To have a really bad day is worse. To have a really bad day when you were supposed to have the best day, and everyone else with their typical families is actually having a great day, well, that's just a real kick to the knackers. It happened time and time again as we struggled through the long day with our emotions tied together with a smile that was always fake.

Karen's sister's wedding: Robyn was supposed to be a
bridesmaid but, as usual, she ended up on my shoulders
eating crisps

But, I suppose, sometimes you have to go there to come back. We had to experience the sheer misery of all those days to know, with complete certainty, that our family was not built for special occasions. It's a lot easier for us, and easier to understand for the host who has issued the partially declined invitation, if everyone has actually witnessed a dozen Dickenson days out go horribly west at almost every attempt. Family and friends have seen more than enough debacles to know that we're not exaggerating. Karen could say in completely good conscience to any invitation, 'Yes, we'd love to come, but it will be just George and me, is that OK?', and everyone would understand. In fact, although they would never say it out loud, they must almost certainly have been relieved that the girls weren't coming to destroy their house and ruin their special day. It was a win for everyone involved, and certainly a win for every member of our family.

Karen could just relax and enjoy the day for what it was without having to constantly check where the girls were, or fear something had happened if we hadn't seen them for two minutes, or deal with a situation where they had destroyed something, apologising over and over and feeling dreadful. George could just hang out with his cousins like a regular kid. He didn't have to be dragged into being a third parent, watching his sisters, or stopping them from doing things they shouldn't be doing, or tearfully joining the search when they had inevitably gone missing.

Robyn and Liberty are usually happiest, and certainly most comfortable, when in their own environment at home. They have all their own toys and entertainment to hand, their food can be supplied whenever they need it, they can go to their own rooms to have a rest if they want to. There's also that state of mind that we all have when we're at home; it's our own place and this is where we're most relaxed. No matter how good a day out or holiday is, who doesn't sigh with relief at getting back to their own house? Or eating their own food how they like it, sitting in their own chairs, and sleeping in their own bed? If that's the case for us, then surely this would go at least double for someone who has a condition where familiarity is key to a peaceful mind? So, which would the girls prefer? Being dragged along to a strange place and interacting (or not interacting) with strange people, where you're constantly being told you can't do the only things that look like they'd be any fun, without many of the things you play with to occupy yourself? Or would you prefer to stay in your own space with everything you need on tap? Something of a no brainer, that one. Yes, ditching the family celebrations was definitely a good move for Robyn and Liberty.

And me? Yes, I was the one who had to miss out on all the special family days. I was the one who had to take care of the girls for a whole day or maybe longer by myself. But they were a lot easier to deal with in their own home. I knew how to keep them safe. I knew I had to keep the doors locked and, as long as I kept hold of the keys, no one else was going to open them and ruin our safety operations. I could make a vat of curry and a big pan of rice and then just heat up their meals in the microwave as and when they shoved dishes and forks in my face. There was never an issue with electronic devices not working, or not having the right film, or a device running out of charge; everything was available and could be plugged in, and they could have the full selection of whatever they wanted to watch or any of their toys. Yes, I would be up and down like a sex worker's proverbials, constantly bringing, fetching, carrying and cooking, but I knew that was the arrangement.

If I could watch a film over the course of an evening while keeping the girls safe and sound and happy, then that was a result for me, too. Sure, it might take four hours to watch a two hour film because of the constant requests for care from one or both of the girls, but that was always understood; I knew that was the deal. It was exasperating at times, and you could start to feel like you had only been put on this earth to act as a servant to two people who couldn't even say thank you or acknowledge your efforts, but it doesn't pay to think about it all too much. This is your job, right now. You have to make your peace with that or you'll just end up very unhappy.

And there was another thing this arrangement gave me. A rather selfish thing. Staying at home with the girls while Karen and George went for the big day out meant I could feel like I was a good dad and a good husband. I was taking one for the team, and I felt good about that. Everybody else was getting the day they wanted, and it pleased me that I was able to be the one who provided that for everyone else. I could be a bit of a martyr: 'No, it's fine, babe. Off you go. You take George and have a really good day. Just relax and enjoy yourself. The girls will be happier here. I've got that film I'm going to try and watch. We'll be OK. Honestly…' It's always sensible to remind your wife once in a while that she made a wise choice marrying you; that you're actually a decent guy and a bit of a keeper.

And being the one who stayed home with the girls also provided me with one last thing: I never wanted to go anyway. Everyone who knows me knows how anti-social I am, and spending a day at home with the girls' constant demands was a small price to pay for skiving something like a wedding. Win.

There was one family wedding, though, that we were all going to have to do our best to attend, and that was when our very own George got married to Dominique a couple of summers back. Had they have got married a year or two before, there wouldn't have been too much of a problem with Robyn and Libby attending as they had become much better behaved in public. However, this was in the middle of the summer of 2018; as you will discover in the next chapter, this was 'Libby's Bad Summer'. At that time, most days were extremely difficult, with frequent meltdowns resulting in Libby attacking her parents at will.

There were lots of preparations for the wedding, but the main worry was the girls behaving, particularly Libby. George obviously had a full understanding of how things were with his sisters, and Dominique had a great rapport with the girls. If there was a kick-off with Libby, no one was going to get upset about it, but everyone was keen to avoid anything unseemly if at all possible.

Libby was at least really looking forward to the wedding, so we were hopeful that her excitement might help to keep her darker moods at bay. She has, of course, seen many, many weddings when watching her Disney and other similar films, so to have a wedding in her own family was something she seemed pretty excited about. Just like with KFC, or other exciting calendar events, the wedding got the full countdown treatment. 'George and Dominique, the wedding day! Three more sleeps!'

Our make-up artist friend Harriet worked wonders

The women of the house were also looking forward to getting the full glamour treatment as Julian the hairdresser came to do their hair, and family friend Harriett came to do make-up. Libby and Robyn both like dressing up and getting make up done. Although Robyn never speaks to tell you she likes dressing up, it's clear that she enjoys having a new dress or a new hairstyle from the amount of times she waltzes off to the mirror to admire herself. And Harriett worked wonders. Robyn always seems to look effortlessly gorgeous, but Libby perhaps needs a little more help. But I couldn't believe how she looked when Harriett had finished. Libby looked absolutely stunning!

To ensure that Robyn was looked after, we invited Hannah, Robyn's carer/friend/guardian angel, to come and sit with her during the service. This meant that Karen and other family members would be available to deal with the clear and present danger of a rampaging Libby at the wedding. As it turned out, Libby was sufficiently happy and excited about the wedding to remain well-behaved but, given the tribulations she caused that summer, we were right to take as many precautions as we could. The only moment where Libby spoke out of turn actually turned out to be rather adorable. During the actual wedding vows, we had this exchange:

Bishop Marzal: Do you, George Bradley Dickenson, take this woman, Dominique Renee Coleman, to be your lawfully wedded wife, to have and to hold, for as long as you both shall live?

George: I do.

Libby: (Loudly) I do!

Far from ruining the mood in any way, it was a lovely little quirky moment that illustrated what it's like to be a member our family. Dominique greeted Libby's outburst with a smile and George put his hand in the air and gave Libby a big thumbs up.

The girls stayed for some of the reception and then we had arranged for them to be taken out for the rest of the day. Local social services provided carers who came to the church to take Libby, and Hannah had a day of activities arranged with Robyn. It was one of the days that could have been a typical family disaster, but went as well as we had any right to hope. Having grown up with the girls and experienced the serious downsides as well as the positives of our family life, it was the least George deserved.

Libby with the bride and groom

DEATH BY A THOUSAND CUTS - LIBERTY'S ILLNESS

PRESENT DAY

The summer of 2018 was one to remember, as much as we wish we could forget it. Everyday was a physical and emotional battle with Liberty. She was clearly unwell and in great pain without the vocabulary to describe that pain, or the mental capacity to process what was happening to her. The only thing she felt she could do to express herself was self-harm and lash out at those around her.

I kept notes on my phone from around this time, like a sort of diary, so I can be fairly certain of the accuracy of my retelling of these events. Even at the time, I described the situation as 'horrific'. I wrote, *'We have been really struggling with her for several weeks as her outbursts have become more and more frequent, prolonged, intense and violent. A dozen full on meltdowns a day is not unusual. Karen and I are covered in bruises, cuts and scratches. Her attacks are physically frightening and emotionally damaging. Having your child more or less beat you up so many times a day is devastating.'*

It's all pretty sobering looking back. I remember it being awful, but my writings from the time suggest it was worse than I remember.

Around this time, Liberty changed her sleeping habits; instead of going to bed of an evening and getting up in the morning as people usually do, she was just sleeping on demand. She did sleep, but she slept as and when she needed to, regardless of the time of day or night. Although she could never explain why, we've always been able to see that stomach pains were a huge part of her issues, and this would contribute to her poor quality of sleep. We would be in our own bedroom, sleeping while we could, but subconsciously knowing that our sleep could be interrupted at any moment.

The first hint you'd get of what was to come would be a faint click from the landing as the light was switched on. That might be enough for a brain already prepared for an attack to begin to rouse itself from its hazy slumber. But if it didn't, the huge crash that came next certainly would. Libby wasn't going to just push the door open; her entrance to our bedroom in the middle of the night always contained a violence that foreshadowed why she was entering. The door would crash into the wall as she smashed it open. As it was just a stud wall, there is still a gaping wound behind the door that we've never bothered to fix; we still have the occasional less than silent night that begins like this from time to time.

Then, after the thump of the door and the crash as it collided with the wall, comes the guttural moan that lets you know that Libby is in pain and, let there be no doubt, she is going to take it out on you. The moan is accompanied by five stomping steps as she traverses the short distance from bedroom door to my side of the bed.

I always sleep on the side of the bed that is nearest the door. If we sleep in a hotel room, I don't choose right or left side, I choose the side nearest the door. I always joked with Karen that this was chivalry; by being closest to the door I would be first to meet any intruder that might enter our room. I would be first to meet the enemy and defend my woman! What a guy! However, my therapist has since told me that I always sleep nearest the door so I can be first to escape in any sort of difficulty. Not such a great guy after all.

So, in our bedroom, I am nearest the door, and thus, nearest to the rampaging Libby.

Five steps. Five quick, loud stomps. That's the time I have to wake up, possibly from deep sleep, and assume a position of defence. First, I need to make sure the duvet is covering me properly. I often get hot in the night, so partially flinging the covers off me in my sleep is part of the cooling system I have developed. But that quilt adds a sturdy layer of protection from the coming attack, so I need to make sure I am covered. Secondly, I turn onto my side. Think about it. Where would you rather receive the unrelenting blows that are about to rain down on you? On your arms, ribs and thighs? Or your chest, stomach and, let's not be coy about it, testicles? OK, some readers may not have testicles, but you've seen it happen enough to know you wouldn't want to receive a heavy whack to them. And besides, you don't want a thump to the stomach or other tender areas. So, you turn on your side and raise your hands to your head whilst leaving your arms as low as you can to provide some protection to your ribs. You've got about 2-3 seconds to make this happen, all in the fug of an abruptly ended sleep.

Then they come. The hammer blows. Oh sure, you may not think a 17 year old girl packs much of a punch, but you'd be wrong. You might also think that Libby's flat handed hitting technique reduces the impact of said punches and makes them just a slap. But you'd be wrong again. Libby's swings start way back like a golf swing. Then they come down with her full weight on you. If there's any bared skin then you're going to get a hand mark that will remain for days. But even if you've managed to cover yourself, you're still going to get the painful impact. She's a canny fighter, too. Liberty won't just pound your fleshy upper arms. She'll zoom in on those exposed ribs, and when you make the rookie mistake of dropping your arms to protect them, then she'll return up top with a blow to the head. You can move your arms and duck and dive all you like, but she's going to make sure it hurts.

And her pinching? Libby is an expert at pinching. A queen of pinching. If pinching were a Jedi skill, she would be a grand-master and have a position on the Jedi Pinching Council. If pinching were an Olympic event, she could easily represent Team GB. In fact, she would be the team captain and take the gold medal. In fact, if there is life on other planets, we could organise an interplanetary pinching tournament and Libby could take the gold by representing Planet Earth and we could all watch satellite footage of her kicking alien ass. Well, pinching alien ass. Except, she wouldn't actually pinch anyone's ass because buttocks are not an effective pinching area. Libby knows that the effective pinching areas are places like the underside of your forearms, your triceps, your calves, and your inner thighs. Oh dear, this is all so funny because our daughter so effectively beat the hell out of us for months on end! Ha ha! Oh boy...

After Libby has unleashed several slaps and pinches, Karen will have woken up and dived out of bed to make it round to my side to try to restrain Libby, but she'll have landed quite a few destructive blows by the time Karen arrives. The effectiveness of Karen's intervention will depend on the severity of Liberty's mood. If she is ultimately just looking for nurturing reassurance, the attack might end there, and she will just turn into her moth-er's embrace and start to sob; Karen would then be able take her back to her room and cuddle her until she went back to sleep. But, during the dark days of 2018, she wasn't looking for comfort. She was in pain and had no way to express that pain, other than by lashing out at those nearest to her. In the past, it had been Karen who had received the worst of Libby's anger but, that summer, it was her Dad that was going to feel her wrath. That meant pushing Mum away so she could inflict more damage on me, but the attempted restraint would have given me a couple of seconds to at least sit upright on the bed in order to make a better defence of myself. If she clearly wasn't for calming down, then we would make a run for it.

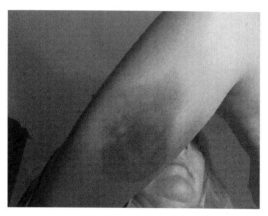

The underside of Karen's arm, displaying Libby's
pinching skills

The best place to hide was the kitchen. All that security that had been implemented to prevent Robyn from escaping was now providing a safe haven for Mum and Dad from a rampaging Libby. If Robyn was around, she would be corralled into the kitchen with us. There's nowhere to sit in the kitchen so, if there was time, you might quickly drag a chair in with you so you didn't have to sit on the floor; we always knew we could be locked in there for the long haul. We also learned that, where possible, it was a really good idea to grab the laptop, your phone and any other fragile yet expensive devices that you see and bring them in the kitchen with us, too. Finally, we would make sure the door was closed and locked and then we would back away to the far side of the kitchen. If Robyn was present, she would just sit with us, looking a little scared but mostly bemused. I don't know what she thought was happening but, then again, she had been on the receiving end of enough nasty injuries at her sister's hands over the years, so maybe she understood all too well.

Libby is bright enough to work the lock on that door. She can write in foreign languages for crying out loud, so she can certainly manage to press '123' then turn the handle. The number code was kept deliberately simple so everyone could use them; the locks were never meant to flummox cat burglars, just Robyn. But we had deliberately never shown Libby how to use them, and now that policy paid off. She would appear at the large, arched, shatterproof window on the kitchen door and start thumping almighty hell out of those windows. As much as one hates to make the parallel of Libby's screaming face pressed up against the window with the scene in The Shining where Jack Nicholson shouts, 'Heeeeere's Johnny!', it is definitely an apposite image to convey what we saw on the other side of that door.

If Libby was just angry, that wasn't so bad; you could sit across the other side of the kitchen and just appeal for her to calm down, not that our appeals ever did much good. However, if she wasn't emotionally upset at the start, she quickly became that way. And so, we would watch through the window, seeing our darling daughter, utterly distraught, thumping the window with everything she had, begging for us to let her in. But so much painfully gained experience had taught us that it was no more wise for us to give in to her cries than it was for the little pigs to let the wolf in.

After a while of getting nowhere, Libby would turn her attention to the rest of the room she was in, that she knew we wouldn't enter. If we hadn't managed to take the vulnerable valuables into the kitchen with us, we would have to watch a little helplessly as she set about them. Expensive phones, iPads, MacBooks, furniture… Hell, eventually we found that that our unbreakable glass in the kitchen door wasn't quite so unbreakable after all. It took a long time, but she cracked it in the end. Hiding in the kitchen could sometimes cost us, or the insurance company, thousands. But we couldn't be fooled. There was no point in going out there or letting her in the kitchen; not at least until we knew she was ready to calm down. That only really came due to exhaustion. When the anger turned to a heartbreaking sadness, then we could start to negotiate a truce. Did she promise there'd be no more pinching and smacking? Was she going to be a good girl now? Until she was ready for that, we were powerless. There was nothing we could do except sit there, watching her scream and cry her frustration, ignoring her pleas, sometimes with tears running down our own faces. We just had to sit and wait for the storm to blow itself out.

DOCTORS DIDN'T SEEM TO HAVE ANY IDEA WHAT WAS WRONG WITH Liberty. They conducted tests, but they always seemed to tell us nothing or be inconclusive. Of course, getting the girls to take tests and other simple medical procedures is always going to be problematic. Despite their difficult early visits that I spoke about in one of my blogs, both girls actually enjoy a trip to the dentist these days. They get to go on the funky chair and have it recline, they put cool glasses on, and Gilly the dentist is fantastic with the girls and is able to make them feel completely at ease. The girls obediently open their mouths and let Gilly prod at their teeth for a while, and will even let her do a bit of a clean and polish. Libby especially likes the rinsing out her mouth and spitting routine after Gilly has finished. So, for checkups, we're fine. However, if something untoward is actually discovered, well, that's going to take a little more effort. That's going to be a trip to the central dentist practice and putting them under general anaesthetic. Even if it's just for a filling.

One of the tests that we had to do for Libby was, obviously, a blood test. Now, I know many adults who have a huge fear of 'needles', so think about trying to explain to someone with so little understanding of the situation that we're about to shove a super sharp piece of metal into their arm and take blood out of them. In fairness to Libby, she was brilliant with this. For a while. The solution to the obvious problem was to apply a local anaesthetic cream to her arm from where the blood was being taken. This would be left on her arm for a while to work its magic, then when the phlebotomist was sure her arm was numb, Karen would distract her by giving her a cuddle from the other side so Libby is looking away from the needle, and then they could extract the blood from her arm. Of course, Libby would never cooperate with something she didn't want to do without seizing the opportunity to secure some treats or presents, so it would have been a case of 'First, go to the doctors and put the cream on your arms, then, McDonald's for three cheeseburgers...' or whatever she'd been promised on this occasion.

This system worked well for a while. But then came Karen's

birthday in 2018. That was the start of one of the worst days of my life. My phone notes of that weekend are very detailed. I assume I kept them to provide evidence for medical staff and social workers. Here's what I wrote, including details of nutrition, medication and violent outbursts.

SATURDAY SEPTEMBER 1 2018

05.45 - 1 x Codeine, 20ml Calpol

Meltdowns at 05.45, 06.30 and 07.30

Libby Slept from 08.00 - 13.15

Holding nose, ears, pressing head together, biting herself, 'sorry for herself' crying, watching sad videos (people dying). Burping.

Woke up at 13.15 - Massive rage. Attacked Barnaby and Karen leaving several nasty bruises.

13.30 - 20mls Calpol and 1 x codeine tablet.

Burping

Shower 14.00 - small outbursts and pinching

14.30 - not happy (noises), small outbursts again, hitting and pinching Barnaby

15.30 - pinching Barnaby

17.00 - attacked Barnaby on the toilet and refused to leave or stop. Continued to cry and be angry upstairs, smashing things.

THE ATTACK ON THE TOILET. OH, I REMEMBER THAT ONE, WELL enough. The indignity! Adults joke about going to the bathroom to take a bit of time out away from their kids, and Mums, particularly, bemoan the fact that even this time is often interrupted by their young kids. But I wasn't just idly sitting on the toilet for a quiet five minutes. I was there to do what I had to do! So, there I am, mid-poo, stressing and straining, physically and emotionally, when in bursts Libby and starts a major attack. If I'd felt vulnerable and unable to escape before when being assaulted, this was a new low; trousers lowered as they should be in such circumstances, stuck on the throne, with your 17 year-old daughter thumping lumps out of you as you cower and pathetically attempt to defend yourself, with, it's safe to say, nowhere to run. I think, in the end, Karen heard the commotion and came and rescued me. I was at least allowed to wipe my bum and pull my trousers back up in order to face the next onslaught...

17.05-17.25 - PROLONGED VICIOUS ATTACK ON BARNABY
 18.00 - 20mls Calpol 1 x Codeine
 20.00 - A few slaps and pinches for Barnaby and Karen
 Libby biting herself
 Took 2 paracetamol
 Ate 1 piece of KFC (first thing eaten today)
 20.15 - 20.30 - Major meltdown. Lots of hitting and pinching.
Nasty bruising for Barnaby and Karen.
 Libby vomits
 22.00 1 x codeine
 Sunday 2nd September
 00.15 Enjoyed back rub and reflexology
 1.20 started to get agitated
 1.25 2 x paracetamol
 1.30 Full blown attack on Barnaby (mostly) and Karen
 More attacks on Karen
 Biting herself, blowing nose a lot, burping.
 2.30 More attacks on Barnaby and Karen
 Codeine x1

AT AROUND 3AM, KAREN DECIDED TO TAKE LIBERTY TO THE ACCIDENT & Emergency department at our local hospital. Because Libby was still in a meltdown when she arrived, she got seen straight away and was put in an isolated room and they were able to start doing tests and X-rays, so this was a big step forward. I had Robyn at home, so I waited until a reasonable hour to get her up and then we headed down to the hospital, stopping along the way to pick up an essential, nutritious breakfast for Libby (a bottle of Pepsi and hot sausage rolls from the garage).

We then had a brief respite as Libby stayed calm for a while. She was entertaining herself watching her YouTube clips on her iPad (seriously, how did people cope before we had these mobile devices?), but now it was time to take some more blood. However, unlike the phlebotomist at our local health centre, the nurse at A&E seemed to be in something of a hurry. The anaesthetic cream was applied but, instead of waiting the appropriate amount of time, they put the needle in her arm before it was numb. It hurt Libby and she pulled her arm away and that was that. Not only did the nurse not get any blood from Libby's arm on this occasion, she had now, for the sake of waiting a few minutes, created fear and something of a phobia that meant that nobody was going to be able to get blood out of her ever again. What had been a fairly simple procedure that Libby was happy to cooperate with had now become some-thing that she was not going to go along with no matter what. Over the next few days we tried on several occasions to get a blood sample, employing all sorts of logic and tricks and promises to get Liberty to cooperate, but no amount of cheese-burgers was going to convince her now she'd been hurt by the needle.

Despite these difficult circumstances, it was still Karen's 48th birthday. Around lunchtime, when Libby had been placed in her own room on the assessment ward, I told Karen to go to my Mum and Dad's nearby, where my Mum had made her a birthday lunch. I stayed with Libby, managing to convince Karen that we were safe in a hospital, I was backed up by all of the hospital staff and everything would be fine if she left Libby with us for a few hours. She could have a nice meal and maybe take a nap on Mum's settee after her sleepless night.

I'm not sorry that I encouraged Karen to go for a rest; it was the right thing to do. And just because Karen had the better relationship with Liberty didn't absolve me of my responsibility to deal with the situation the best that I could, especially on what was supposed to be a special day for her. But, and be assured that this isn't remotely hyperbole, I was about to experience some of the worst hours of my life.

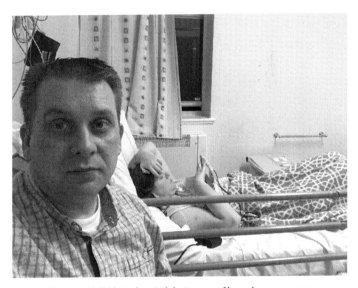

Sitting with Libby in hospital during one of her calmer moments

I don't remember all the details. Damn, in many ways I wish I didn't remember any of them. Bottom line, Libby flipped biggest time. This had happened many times before, and I had dealt with it on my own before, too. But that was on home turf; now we were in a hospital and the whole thing was quite, quite different. I can't remember what she wanted or where she wanted to go, but there was a busy ward full of patients just next to where her private room was, and on the one occasion where she managed to get out of her room, she caused havoc; screaming and shouting and generally playing absolute hell, then hitting anyone who tried to prevent her from doing so.

Once she was back in her room, the goal was to keep her there at all costs. Libby screamed and shouted and punched and pinched and thumped me for several hours. The attacks raged, they ebbed and flowed; Libby would appear to calm herself for a few minutes, but she was really just getting her energy and breath back before launching the next wave of violence. Over the next few hours I developed a bruise on the underside of my forearm that was about ten inches long and four inches wide; it looked like a blunt trauma bruise from a car crash, and that was far from the only injury I sustained. This was exactly why we locked ourselves in the kitchen at home. This was what would happen to us without locked doors in our house. Although, even without the locked doors, at least we could run away at home; there were possible escape routes. There were times when I would just go outside and let her chase me around the garden. I weigh a fair bit more than I did in my younger days, but I can still outrun Libby.

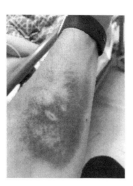

Pinch upon pinch upon pinch leaves you with a bruise on the underside of your forearm like this

Here at the hospital, however, the need to keep Libby in her room meant that I couldn't run anywhere. The nurses on the ward were all trying to back me up, but I felt guilty when they got in the way of Libby's blows. Nursing is a tough gig at the best of times, they certainly didn't need an aggressive 17 year-old assaulting them. So, I was not only between Libby and all of the other patients, but I was also the barrier between Libby and the hospital staff, protecting them from her outbursts, too. There was no one to defend me and, other than trying to restrain her, mostly unsuccessfully, I refused to do anything to physically assault her in order to defend myself.

I can remember standing in the doorway, with my arms out, blocking her exit and defending the medical staff. As she took a pause from her otherwise sustained attack, I had a moment to take things in and the tears just started streaming down my face. In my notes I wrote:

'I just stood there crying, in front of a bunch of strangers, while my daughter beat me up. The tears were long overdue as a release from the last few weeks, but I'd rather that had happened at home.'

It's pretty awful that, on top of everything else, I felt so embarrassed and vulnerable. It may seem obvious to some, though not to all, but I never blamed Liberty for any of this. I knew she was in deep pain; I knew that she had no way of processing or expressing that pain. And I knew none of this was her fault. I'm not trying to tell you I was happy that any of this was happening. There were times when I got angry about her behaviour, and I would shout at her to stop and yell in pain and swear in my own frustration. But I always knew she was blameless. Eventually, when her howling pain and frustration turned to tears of exhaustion, your heart would break for her, as she gave in and just sobbed on her mother's shoulder.

That stage had not been reached yet, though, and this attack seemed angrier and more prolonged and violent than any yet, and she didn't show any sign of letting up. Eventually, the word came down from the senior practitioner on the shift that a sedative could be administered. Bearing in mind that Libby had her first bad experience with needles just that morning, and that had not been when she was heightened, this was not going to be administered easily. Eventually, after various attempts that Libby rebuffed aggressively, it took six of us to pin her down so she could be jabbed in her thigh. It was like a high octane scene from one of those hospital dramas like Casualty or Grey's Anatomy where the hysterical patient is sedated by a whole team of medics. It was sickening to be a part of, and deeply sobering to realise that this was happening in real life to my lovely, sweet girl, who wanted nothing more than to watch the movies she loved, eat KFC and draw pictures of Disney Princesses before this had all started.

As Libby started to become drowsy, the nurses behind me began to back away out of her room. I moved the chair from next to Libby's bed and placed it in the doorway, just to have that barrier between Libby and everyone else, just in case. As the uneasy calm began to settle after the tempest that we'd been through, I allowed myself to sit and just sob my heart out. It was an awful moment. Yes, a few hours of time had been bought via pharmaceutical intervention, but it would soon start again, and we weren't seeing any way out. We could expect more of the same, and soon.

The next morning, Karen and I were both present as Liberty started to go into meltdown again. As it was now a Monday, the Senior Nurse of the ward was back on shift and was trying to help us contain the situation. Libby quickly returned to the dizzying heights of attack from the previous afternoon.

There was talk among the nurses of calling the police; quite what they thought the local constabulary were going to do to alleviate the situation, I'm not sure, but it gives you some idea of how even hardened professionals were at a loss as to what to do. When Libby first started to 'go up', we told the senior nurse how the staff had given her a sedative the previous afternoon. The nurse explained to us how this action had gone completely against protocol and couldn't possibly happen again. Then, about 15 minutes later, I helped various nurses pin Liberty down so the same Senior Nurse could administer another sedative to our daughter. Exactly like she'd sworn we couldn't do just 15 minutes earlier.

This seemed a common reaction amongst doctors, nurses and specialists that we dealt with. Their responses when we described Libby's symptoms and behaviours were glib and inadequate. Then, when they witnessed her behaviour first hand, the penny dropped. They began to take the situation seriously and start to prescribe more serious medication, and try to fast track other treatment. It happened time and time again. I wrote in my notes at the time:

'The bottom line is, no one can control Libby. Even in hospital she is completely out of control. We can't ask anybody else to take responsibility for her, especially not the usual allies like our fairly elderly parents. So Karen and I have had to deal with Libby more or less 24/7 for the last few weeks. It isn't that we know how to calm her down; we don't. We don't have the remedy either. It's just we can't expect anybody else to put themselves in harm's way.

Libby is sedated right now, but this morning's meltdown was pretty traumatic and Karen and I are getting close to breaking point. I haven't gone back to work today - how could I? When will Karen sleep if I don't take a shift with Libby? The hardest thing is not being able to ask anyone to help. Because nobody should have to go through this. Including Liberty. Bless her.'

Later the next day, the medical team explained that they thought that Libby had experienced an infection that had stoked the fires of her behaviour. As the prescribed antibiotics fought the infection, Libby became calmer and we were able to take her home. But if we thought that we were completely out of the woods with our youngest daughter, we thought wrong.

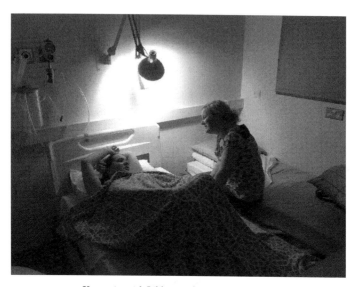

Karen sits with Libby on a later stay in hospital

I COULD PROBABLY TELL MANY STORIES AN AWFUL LOT LIKE THIS ONE to give you the full picture of what 2018 and early 2019 was like for Liberty and our family. But, for me at least, Karen's 48th birthday serves as an appropriate snapshot for that part of our lives.

There are many more details I could give, but I'll cut to the chase. No real diagnosis of Libby's overall issues have ever been made. However, she was given more medication than a doctor could shake a stethoscope at and, over time, some of this helped alleviate her stomach pain. Those pains do persist at times, albeit less seriously, and with less violent outcomes. Stomach and bowel problems are an odd but very common feature of people with autism. More from my notes:

'It's a slightly bizarre symptom of autism, but many people with the condition also suffer from bowel issues. I won't bore you (or gross you out) with the details, but it's enough to say that Liberty has some major issues that cause her (and would cause anyone) a lot of pain. In fact, doctors have told us that most adults wouldn't be able to deal with the pain that Libby must be in.'

We also conceded that, for the first time, we would have to give one of our daughters serious medication to help control her pain and her moods. Firstly, she had to take eight sachets of Movicol everyday. Movicol is a laxative treatment for adults which Libby was now taking to begin to ease her bowel issues, but eight sachets a day is a pretty big dose. It's also a powder that is mixed in water, so we mixed Vimto fruit cordial into the mix, too, to make it palatable for her. Libby was always treated with a few Cadbury's chocolate buttons after she'd necked her glass of special Movicol cocktail in order to take the taste away. She was prescribed Risperidone, too, an anti-psychotic drug, often used to treat schizophrenia in adults, but it was given to Libby to reduce her agitation.

Among other medication, Libby also had a prescription for Lorazepam, which is a benzodiazepine in the same pharmaceutical group as Valium. When Libby could no longer attend school because of her behaviour, Lorazepam was the support we were given instead. Basically, if you decide you can't take any more violence from your kid, get her to take this stuff. Lorazepam was now our respite. At her residence they will still use Lorazepam sometimes, as it's how you can stop a Libby meltdown. However, we have rarely used it at home because it just turns Libby into a zombie. We hate how it must make her feel; she is so obviously not even the same person when she takes Lorazepam. We also hate how it makes us feel. I know how harsh this sounds, but if you ever want to feel heartbroken and like a failing parent at the same time, give your child Lorazepam.

I totally appreciate that it may be necessary for some people at times, as it was for us and still is necessary for Libby at her residence occasionally, but it was always a tough call. We had always shied away from using medication to treat our girls, but times had clearly changed. When we finally left the hospital, we walked out with a shopping bag full of controlled substances that would make your local shady dealer green with envy.

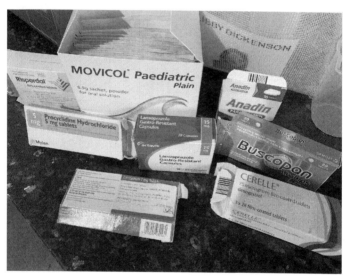

Libby's array of medication

IN MARCH 2019, HAVING ONLY TURNED 18 JUST A FEW MONTHS previously, Libby moved out of our family home to a residential unit for adults with additional needs and behavioural issues; her new home was about 45 minutes from where we live. Everyone did their best to ensure a smooth transition for Libby, but nothing could prepare us as parents for the first time we would have to say goodbye to our brave little girl and just leave her on her own with only carers for company. We would visit many times before either of us could say goodbye to her without walking back to the car in tears.

All of this happened to Karen as much or more than it happened to me. And even though our story is shared, this is ultimately the story as I see it. And I have to accept that 2018 broke me. We dealt with so much as we raised our girls, and were willing and often happy to do so. But, I guess everyone has a limit. Everyone has a point where they can go no further. Everyone, no matter who they are, sooner or later, has a breaking point, and looking back, I can see that this was mine.

We had to accept more than just a little help here and there with Libby. We had to let someone else take care of her needs day to day. The teaching job that had financially supported us through all of this time, and also allowed me to be home during weekends and holidays so Karen didn't have to do it by herself, well, that also ended about the same time that Libby moved out. I'd always found it a stressful occupation, but after 20 years it just stopped dead. I left the school building one day in the middle of the spring term and told myself I wasn't going back. I don't think it was a coincidence that all of this happened at the same time. I'm writing this three years later, and it's very clear to me that this was as much as I could take. Either we made changes in our lives, or I was going to go under. Writing about this time brings so many feelings back, and some of these choices were heartbreakingly difficult. But this was what we had to do for the best for everyone involved. With the benefit of hindsight, I look back and know that we really had no choice.

❧ 14 ❧

SOON YOU'LL GET BETTER - COVID-19

PRESENT DAY

And so, due to her poor health and the extreme behaviours that resulted from it, Liberty moved to a residential care home and, ten months later, Robyn also moved into a full time care residence. It's slightly odd that Robyn was almost 22 when she moved out and Libby was barely 18, but that reflects their different circumstances. Libby had to move away from home because of the difficulties that she was experiencing and also causing for us. She had been forced to leave high school with almost two years left to run as staff just couldn't deal with her anymore. It also meant that she did not have the opportunity to attend college after high school. Robyn did not have those issues, and so had been able to stay in high school until she was 19 and then do two years in college before Social Services had to even think about finding a full time residence for her.

Libby's new place was called Oak and was quite clearly an institution, albeit a very nice one. The building itself was made of wood and glass and very modern and was shared with up to seven other residents, usually all male, though each resident had one to one supervision and care. The residence itself was part of a larger campus with quite a few different homes, and Libby eventually moved to one of the smaller places after spending about 15 months at Oak.

Libby in her new room at Oak

Robyn's place was much more like an actual house. In fact, it was actually two semi-detached houses knocked into one residence. Like Libby, Robyn had her own bedroom and shared the house with three other adult females, all of whom had autism to the extent that they could not ordinarily function in mainstream society without significant support. When Robyn moved out, the circumstances were quite different to Libby. Robyn wasn't being moved out as an emergency due to her violent behaviour. It was simply time.

As I said, she was nearly 22, and 22 year-olds don't live with their parents. Well, that used to be the case before young people were priced out of the housing market. Karen and I actually bought our first house when we were both 21, so you get the idea. However, it was still heartbreaking leaving her there for the first time, and for the first few times that we dropped her back there after visits home. She'd stayed away from home plenty of times before. From the time she was 8 she had stayed at the residential annexe at school two nights a week, then gone onto college where she only came home at the weekend and during school holidays, but this felt different. And it felt different because it was permanent. We still see Robyn very frequently. Unlike Libby, Robyn only lives 10 minutes from our house. She comes home every other weekend, and on the alternate Saturdays we take her out for the day with her sister for KFC. And if I'm off work on a Wednesday, as I often am, I'll pick her up and take her out then, too. So, she gets to see us a lot.

Robyn in her bedroom at her residence

But, if I'm honest, I'd rather she was just at home with us all the time. It seems to me that this is where she is happiest and most comfortable. It's not really possible, though, and it's not fair, either. Robyn moving out meant that Karen was able to return to the world of work after 25 years of being a stay at home mum, and she felt that was something she wanted to do. We also have to acknowledge that we just can't give Robyn, or Libby, the kind of one to one constant care and attention they get at their residences. If she's at home with us then she gets cared for, of course she does, but we have to cook, clean and maintain our own home. We also need to be able to take time to relax ourselves while we're not at work. Whereas the people looking after the girls are actually at work; giving the girls their full attention is what they're paid to do.

So, in the early days of the girls moving out, we found it emotional and difficult. We had to adapt to this new situation knowing that, in the long run, things would likely be better for all of us. Something else was about to come along, though. Something that was going to make everything tougher for everyone. COVID-19.

The first lockdown was rough on all of us, wasn't it? None of us had experienced anything quite like this. We were all in uncharted territory, navigating strange waters, wearing masks, staying home, daily walks, Zoom calls, baking banana bread, exercising with Joe Wicks... it was all very odd. But imagine you've got to deal with the isolation and change without the first understanding of why it's happening. Now imagine that possibly your favourite thing in the world is spending time with your family, and suddenly you're no longer allowed to do that. That's what happened to Robyn and Libby at different times.

Libby's care home initially allowed her to come home, but the company who run Robyn's home had different procedures. She was not allowed to come home and was not allowed to have any visitors. The most we could do was go to her home and talk to her through a partially opened window. As I've said previously, you can't have casual conversations with Robyn. She doesn't speak, and so the best way of communicating with her is through tone and expression, very much up close. This wasn't possible at all, so we were left just trying to somehow get her attention through a crack in a window. I can still recall how she looked at us with an expression that just seemed to say, 'Dad, what are you doing? Why are you out there? Just come in and get me and take me home with you!' The only time I managed to really make a breakthrough and make her laugh was when I sang her the whole of the song 'Poor Unfortunate Souls' from The Little Mermaid. That worked one time, but very little else did. Oh, but it was heartbreaking. And worse was to come.

In new or difficult situations, it's common for autistic people to do things in order to give themselves control of their situation. Some might not behave in a usual way, or start a new behaviour, or some might stop eating. Robyn stops going to the toilet; specifically, Robyn stops pooing. I have no idea how someone does that for more than a few hours after they feel they need to go, and I'd imagine it's the same for you, but this is common for Robyn when she is away from home. When she went to college, she would never go for a number two, waiting instead until she came home for the weekend. Then she would arrive home and head straight for the downstairs bathroom and indulge in what I rather uncouthly began to refer to as Robyn's Friday Night… well, it rhymed with 'night'. But there was at least fair reason for my vulgarity as I was paying a rather unpleasant price for this habit.

At the time I was trying to lose weight, and so I would often get home from work and get on the treadmill that we keep in the girls' playroom. I always ran on a Friday when I got in from work to make a good start to the weekend, but also so I could then get a shower and relax and enjoy Friday night. So, I'd be pounding the moving pavement, in the zone, in the middle of a good 10K run, when in would burst Robyn, straight past my treadmill, straight into the downstairs bathroom to evacuate her bowels for the first time in a week. Often without closing the door. Seriously, have you ever tried to do a serious run, taking those big gulps of air and, 5K in, someone comes in and literally takes a dump so that's all you can breathe for the rest of your run? Robyn, you're my special girl and I love you, but I always loved you just a little less on those Friday evenings.

Telling that story has reminded me of another habit Robyn had in this regard; one that was just plain bizarre as well as anti-social. Like a lot of students with additional needs, Robyn and Libby were provided with a taxi to take them to school. This was particularly helpful for our girls as they went to a specialist school for kids with autism that was about 45 minutes from our home. When they arrived home from school, Karen would go out to the car to have a quick chat with their escort who travelled with them every day, just to check in and make sure everything was OK. In the time that Robyn had while her Mum was busy, she would run up the stairs, enter her own bedroom, climb to the top of the five foot high chest of drawers that stored her clothes, and this would be the place that she chose, whenever she could at the end of the school day, to go for a poo. On top of the chest of drawers. I am not exaggerating when I tell you that the toilet in the bathroom was less than six feet away from the very spot that she had chosen to curl one out. But why go to the toilet that's got a built in seat where you can flush everything away, when you can go on the chest of drawers, smear some around your bedroom, and create a sizeable, disgusting mess for Mum or Dad to have to clean up? Where's the fun in going to a boring old toilet to do your business?

Anyway, I need to return to a story that, believe it or not, couldn't be much more serious. Robyn's refusal to go to the toilet was becoming a major issue. Whilst not ideal, when she was visiting home a couple of times a week, it wasn't such a problem. She would simply hold on for a few days, then go to the loo when she came home. As long as I wasn't on the tread-mill at the time, this way of doing things more or less worked. But with the COVID restrictions, Robyn wasn't coming home at all. As time went on, the situation got more and more serious.

BARNABY DICKENSON

We reached seven weeks and Robyn still hadn't gone to the toilet. We visited her in that seventh week and noticed that she was in such discomfort that she couldn't even sit down properly. She looked pale, listless, and very unhappy.

On the Saturday morning, the manager of Robyn's house called us and asked us to come and get Robyn and bring her home. Taking precautions against COVID is all well and good, but these restrictions were making Robyn very ill right here and now. When I picked her up that morning, I took a photo of her that we still have, and she looks awful. Then I have a photo of her from about an hour later. She is sitting in the sunshine in 'her spot' on the oil tank in our back garden, sunglasses on, skin already looking a healthier colour, with a great beaming smile on her face. It's what happened in that hour between the photos that proved controversial.

Robyn - Before and after

Believe me when I tell you that you don't need the gory details of what happened in the interim, but not moving your bowels for 7 weeks has consequences, and so Karen helped Robyn to go. Nothing 'invasive' was done, just a bit of pressing around the area to get things going and then Robyn could get the job done and go back to being our happy little girl. Several days later, Karen was telling this story to someone from the management office of the company that ran Robyn's home. We were extremely surprised by their response to the situation.

'Did you have permission from a medical professional to help Robyn's bowel movement?' I'm sorry, how does that work? I can understand that, as parents and legal guardians of someone who cannot give their own consent, a medical professional might seek our permission to do something, but since when did we have to ask someone who doesn't even know Robyn if we can do something as straight forward as help her to go to the toilet? Well, it turns out that, because Robyn was now an adult, we did need permission. It also turns out that these sorts of things are taken very seriously.

The situation was reported to social services and they made the decision that we were no longer allowed to keep Robyn at home. That's right. Robyn had been in a home where she had become ill. We had brought her home and resolved the situation through entirely reasonable means. And now we were being adjudged to not be responsible enough to care for our own daughter? And she was being returned to where she had become ill, now that we had solved the problem for them? After all we had been through with our daughters, now social services were taking our daughter away?

I was beyond upset and a long way past angry. People often don't behave reasonably when they perceive the safety of their children is threatened, and I found out that I'm no exception. Quite simply, I wasn't going to allow it to happen. We had done nothing wrong, Karen had done what any caring mother of a special needs person would do, and they weren't taking Robyn. Over my dead body. I was told that the police would have to get involved and my attitude was 'bring them on'. As I've told you before, I'm no fighter, and am not in the least bit macho. And yet, here I was, suddenly anxious to stand up to the police and willing to be arrested.

It wasn't until someone pointed out to me that all this posturing was pointless that I started to calm down. The police would be involved if I didn't let Robyn go, they would arrest me, and then social services would take Robyn anyway, so there was absolutely nothing to be gained by refusing to cooperate. I arranged to just take Robyn back to her house myself, rather than go through the trauma of social services physically dragging her away. Taking her back myself wasn't much better; I was an emotional mess as I dropped her off and drove home.

Unsurprisingly, once the case was investigated and we had made our views on the subject clear, there wasn't a case to answer. But this served as an insight into the power of social services and how there are times as a parent that you really need to fight for the rights of your child and your rights as a parent. I understand that there are rules and procedures that social services have to follow, and those involved are just doing their job, but when you have sacrificed so much for your children and done all you can for them for decades despite the circumstances, it was a situation that was tough to take.

In the early days of COVID, Libby was allowed to come home and Robyn wasn't. As lockdown rules changed and there were some positive cases among the staff at Libby's house, the situation reversed. Libby does have a better understanding of things happening around us than Robyn, but that understanding is still fairly limited. Staff tried to explain to Libby, using simple explanations and pictures, that there were 'germs' that would make Libby very poorly. She understood it a little bit but, when there was a positive case in her house and we were not allowed in and she was not allowed out to see us, that understanding was considerably stretched. Once again, our contact with one of our daughters was limited to talking through an open window. We've got phone footage that shows her banging against the window trying to get out as we stood there, rather hopelessly trying to explain why she couldn't come out.

There seemed to be a lot of inconsistency about who was allowed to go where and when during lockdown, a lot of which was down to the interpretation of lockdown rules by the homes themselves, rather than government guidelines. We could do FaceTime calls with Libby on her iPad, though, and that helped to be able to have simple conversations and act out scenes from films with Mum and Dad. In theory we could have done the same with Robyn, and we did try a few times, but Robyn doesn't talk back, and with a completely one sided conversation, there seemed little point.

Communicating with their parents through a crack in a window was as good as it got for our daughters at times during COVID

In order to appease Libby, we arranged for her to have presents at the weekend that we would take for her instead of her coming home. These could be put on her calendar to give her something to look forward to. It was the usual array of DVDs, soundtrack CDs, and various merchandise from her favourite films. This helped bridge the emotional gap of not being able to see her Mum. When lockdown restrictions eased, we were able to see Libby again and she was able to come back home at weekends. But if you think that meant the end of Libby's weekly presents, then you're underestimating Libby's street smarts. We're 15 months on from all that now, and Libby still gets a present of her choosing put on her calendar every weekend. Sharp as a tack, that girl.

Libby shows us one of her weekly presents during one of our FaceTime calls

Libby's Mum is pretty sharp, too. As lockdown began to loom there were rumours about how and when it was going to happen. Initially there were requests made from the government before there was a complete shutdown. Karen had a few concerns about how lockdown was going to affect the girls, particularly if certain businesses were closed. On 16th March 2020, when Prime Minister Boris Johnson made the first initial lockdown, suggesting that people shouldn't go to bars or restaurants, Karen was putting her coat on before Boris had even finished his press conference. 'Where are you off to?' I asked. 'KFC', she replied.

Karen and Robyn visit Libby during COVID

She returned half an hour later with three buckets of KFC boned chicken and some empty unused KFC boxes. After she'd let them cool, she then divided them into portions of three pieces, wrapped them up and put them in the freezer. KFC might have been about to close their doors for the next few months, but there was no way that Libby was going to be able to understand that. She'd be wanting her KFC every Saturday, lockdown or not. And Karen was thinking ahead. So every Saturday, Karen could take a pack of KFC from the freezer, cook them in the oven, then put them in one of the boxes that she had been kindly given by the KFC staff when she had explained why we needed them. Even if we weren't able to take Libby out on the Saturday, or she hadn't come home, we could deliver her KFC to Oak House where she lived. She never had to miss a single Saturday of having her favourite fried chicken during the whole of lockdown. Clever Mummy.

Karen gets the batches of fried chicken ready for freezing

❧ 15 ❧

CLOSURE

I actually could go on, but I need to stop somewhere. Three days ago I drew a line in the sand and said, 'That's it. That's the end.' Since then I've remembered another nine stories that I could tell, and I'm pretty sure that pattern would continue and I will remember dozens more. Maybe I can write a sequel sometime in the future, but if I ever want to finish this book, I have to end it somewhere, and this is where I have chosen to stop. I think you've got the idea about what our life has been like for the past 22 years. Plus, with both girls moving out and the issues brought about by COVID which, fingers crossed, are largely behind us now, it seems a logical time to conclude. We have reached the end of our daughters' childhoods.

There's a strange thing, though, that happened to me as I wrote the newer stories over the last couple of months. I had to relive some of the most difficult days of my life in fine detail. We don't normally do that. Memories and feelings flit about in our heads, but we don't sit down and try to remember and recount all the specifics. Especially not difficult memories: Karen's birthday in 2018 when Liberty beat me black and blue at the hospital and then I had to help pin her down so she could be sedated; social services taking Robyn away from us; being kept away from our daughters because of the rules around COVID, just standing outside their houses waving and blowing kisses to them while they just gawped at us, uncomprehending. You don't dwell on those kinds of memories unless you have to.

And as I've reread and edited the early blogs, it's clear that the challenges we faced when the girls were younger have become very different challenges as they have got older. It's easy for Karen and me to forget how difficult they were in their younger years. Robyn; our beautiful, placid Robyn, who barely causes us a moment's trouble, was entirely relentless back then. If you took your eyes off her for one minute you were asking for trouble that she would invariably provide. It was exhausting. And writing all about Liberty's recent illness has brought it all back into my mind, front and centre. Good grief, that pair have been a handful over the years, and I don't doubt that it has come at some cost to our well being.

But as I sat at my laptop and wrote about my daughters while they are away in their new homes, all these memories came dancing back into my head, lurid and bright once more, and there was only one reaction in my heart; I couldn't wait to see my girls to hold them again. When they came home at the weekends, I realised that writing about them had, in a strange way, reminded me of just how much I love them. Writing these memories down has just brought me even closer to Robyn and Libby. They are at their new residences for much of the time now, but when I think about them, I rarely think about the difficulties they used to bring and sometimes still do. I just think about how much I adore them.

I do sometimes wonder, though, what our lives might have been like if our girls were just plain old vanilla neurotypical. What would George's life have been like? As I wondered ten years ago when Robyn turned 13, how would it have been to walk my girls down the aisle at their wedding, or go with them to get their exam results, or to attend their university graduation and watch them throw their caps in the air? There are no guarantees that either of my daughters would have done any of those things, but when I see other families experiencing those rites of passage and special occasions, it does make my heart ache a little. It probably doesn't cross those parents' minds just how blessed they are.

I am one of seven children and Karen is one of five. When George and Robyn were small, and Karen was expecting Liberty, we were not thinking that we would only have three children. We were very much enjoying our young family and we both wanted a big family like the ones we grew up in. Somewhere out there on a road not travelled are our children that we didn't have. We couldn't have them. It wouldn't have been fair to them, or to our autistic daughters, or to George.

And what guarantee was there that they would have been in any way typical? We were struggling to cope with the amount of autism in our home already; Robyn and Liberty gave us more than enough to deal with. And so, there is that idea out there of the children that we wanted, but will never have. I know that happens to lots of other people, too; we are not special for being deprived of having children we would have liked to have. But the reasons for that with other people are usually biological, rather than neurological. What would Dickenson child number four or five have been like? They would have been as fabulous as the other three, I'm sure. But we'll never know. We'll never meet them. I wouldn't want to give the impression that this is something I dwell on every day, because it isn't. But it is something I reflect on from time to time, and is a cause of heartbreak and sadness for me.

Would we have been happier if our daughters were not autistic? A philosophical observation you are already aware I like to make is that when our circumstances in life change, then we trade one set of problems for another set of problems. There are precious few problem free situations, and surely no problem free children. Our lives would have been very different if Robyn and Liberty had not been autistic, of that there can be no doubt. But there are no guarantees that our lives would have been 'better'. There are all kinds of problems that most parents have to deal with as they raise their daughters that have never crossed our paths. There have been none of the usual battles about curfews and parties and skirt lengths. And oh, how I would have hated their boyfriends or husbands. Based on my relationship with my father-in-law, I'm pretty sure that's my job. Who cares about your credentials, sunshine, that's my daughter and you'll never be good enough for her! Well, the universe spared me from being that guy, at least.

As I have said before, my little girls have stayed my little girls, no matter what age they are, and there is something wonderful about that. Imagine it this way: if you're a parent, how would you feel about your child staying a toddler forever? Because that's kind of where our girls are at. It would be a mixed blessing, right? They would be gorgeous and adorable, but you would always feel sad that they never got to reach their full potential; you would watch them grow physically older, but know that mentally and emotionally they would never grow up. And I suppose that's where we're at as parents.

But there is a beauty and a simplicity to my relationship with my daughters that is unlikely to change too much now. Despite everything I have just said, you shouldn't think that I sit around on a day-to-day basis bemoaning my lot, or deeply reflecting on the life that both the girls and I haven't lived. I rarely do that. I'm far too busy making my girls curry, quoting The Goonies with Libby, singing to Robyn, doing my best to make them smile, because that's what makes me smile.

No one gets a perfect shot at life. No one gets to live in a permanent state of grace. And I can't lie and declare that this is the life I would have chosen if such a choice was offered. But I have a beautiful, clever and incredibly supportive wife who continues to be the most amazing mother to our children in circumstances that have, at times, been close to impossible. She has helped to preserve my delicate sanity when our collective tribulations threatened to pull me under. I have my eldest, our remarkable and brave child, who I often refer to as 'the one who talks to me' and now, in their mid-twenties, has become a friend and confidante for which I am blessed and grateful. And I have two daughters that have taught me so much. The father that they were given may not have been entirely up to the task, but I know all too well that they have helped to make me a better father and a better man. They do so much that makes me happy that it would be churlish to feel anything but grateful for the life that I have been given. I look at my family and, far from feeling neglected and cursed, I know that I am the lucky one. True, there is much in our story that has been sad and seemingly tragic, but this is all part of the tapestry that we weave that makes life worth living.

So, if their childhood is over now, then, reflecting on this book's title, my daughters have failed in their bid to kill me. But I do still love them. Oh, how I love them. Forever and always.

ACKNOWLEDGMENTS

To Rachel (Ginger), Ruby, Gilly, Viv, Hannah, Dominique, (Aunt) Sarah, Virginia, Auntie Barbara, Uncle Nick, Georgia, Joely, and all those who have taken a special interest in our gorgeous girls. Thank you. Your support has always been appreciated.

To Natalie - For all your help in 'post-production' and all your support, encouragement and belief. Thank you.

To Kate & Spike - For being frequent co-stars of this book and for returning our calls at times when other people might have conveniently lost our number.

To the members of IQLBA - You're a select bunch, but with amazing taste. Thank you for sticking with this miserable old git. There must be easier people to have as a friend. Love you.

To G - Thank you for your support and understanding and for being the child that talks to me. Never think that because I didn't write a book about you that I loved you any less!

To my Facebook posse - Thank you for constantly believing in me and sending me supportive messages when I wanted to throw my toys out of the pram. Also, for all your feedback when we got to the post-production stage. It gave me the confidence to get this book out there.

To Mark G - Thank you for inspiring me.

To COVID-19 - Ten days in the house on my own feeling rubbish with nothing to do really helped me break the back of writing this book. It was the only good thing about you.

To Grandy, Gramps, Grandma & Grandad - Not just for being great grandparents, but in your willingness to take care of the girls to give us time out and help our marriage to survive. Thank you.

To my gorgeous, funny, clever girls, Liberty Belle and Beanie Pie - Daddy loves you.

Barnaby Dickenson spent twenty years as a high school English teacher, so at least grammatical errors in this book should be fairly thin on the ground. He is a father of three children, two of whom have autism. He is a fan of Apple (but not apples), rubbish Christmas movies, Nike Air Force One shoes, Taylor Swift and Mountain Dew. This is his first book. It took ten years to write, so look out for the sequel in 2031.